Property with She's *on the* M●ney

Victoria Devine is transforming the way millennials think about money. With a background in behavioural psychology and chart-topping podcasts, *She's on the Money* and *The Property Playbook*, Victoria understands what makes her generation tick and she knows how to make hard-to-understand concepts fun, fresh and relatable.

Now retired from her role as an award-winning financial adviser, Victoria is a co-director and founder of Zella Money, an award-winning mortgage-broking business, and a financial columnist for *The Age* and *Sydney Morning Herald*. She has been a guest speaker at events and featured in publications such as *The Financial Standard*, *Vogue*, ABC News, RMIT Future of Financial Planning, Mamamia, *Elle* magazine, Yahoo Finance and many more. She was also named on the *Forbes* 30 Under 30 Asia list for 2021.

Victoria's number one bestselling first book, *She's on the Money*, won the ABIA General Non-fiction Book of the Year 2022 and the Best Personal Finance & Investment Book of the Year at the 2021 Business Book Awards.

If you can't find her, chances are she's at home with an oat latte in one hand and her Old English sheepadoodle, Lucy, in the other.

shesonthemoney.com.au

○ @shesonthemoneyaus

f @ShesontheMoneyAUS

Also by Victoria Devine

She's on the Money
Investing with She's on the Money
She's on the Money Budget Journal

The ultimate first
home buyer's guide

Property
with
She's
on the
Money

Victoria Devine

LIFE

PENGUIN LIFE

UK | USA | Canada | Ireland | Australia
India | New Zealand | South Africa | China

Penguin Life is part of the Penguin Random House group of companies
whose addresses can be found at global.penguinrandomhouse.com

Penguin
Random House
Australia

First published by Penguin Life in 2023

Cover and text design by Alissa Dinallo © Penguin Random House Australia Pty Ltd
Illustrations by Louisa Maggio © Penguin Random House Australia Pty Ltd
Author photograph by Miranda Stokke
Typeset in 10.5/14 pt Mercury Text by Post Pre-press Group, Australia

Printed and bound in Australia by Griffin Press, an accredited
ISO AS/NZS 14001 Environmental Management Systems printer

 A catalogue record for this
book is available from the
National Library of Australia

ISBN 978 0 14377 877 6

penguin.com.au

MIX
Paper | Supporting
responsible forestry
FSC® C018684

We at Penguin Random House Australia acknowledge that Aboriginal and Torres
Strait Islander peoples are the Traditional Custodians and the first storytellers
of the lands on which we live and work. We honour Aboriginal and Torres
Strait Islander peoples' continuous connection to Country, waters, skies and
communities. We celebrate Aboriginal and Torres Strait Islander stories, traditions
and living cultures; and we pay our respects to Elders past and present.

As the author of this book I'd like to acknowledge and pay respect to Australia's Aboriginal and Torres Strait Islander peoples, the traditional custodians of lands, waterways and skies across Australia. I'd like to particularly acknowledge the Wurundjeri people of the Kulin Nation who are the traditional custodians of the land on which I was able to write this book. I pay my respects to Elders past and present, and I share my friendship and kindness.

For *you*. I'm so proud of where you've come from, and I'm so excited to see where you're going to go.

Contents

Prologue

Hi, hello and welcome to She's on the Money! It's so lovely to have you here. I'm so humbled that our community has grown from a little-known Facebook group and podcast begun in 2019 to a powerful collective willing to share their struggles, stories and wins to inspire others. Our millennial go-getters transform their approach to money by following the hot tips, money wins and resources available through the She's on the Money books, podcasts, Insta and real-life affiliated services such as my mortgage-broking firm, Zella Money.

I am Victoria Devine, a neuro-spicy, animal-loving, Melbourne-based millennial. I used to be a practising financial adviser, but nowadays I focus more broadly on helping others find ways to enjoy money wins and avoid unnecessary money pitfalls. In late 2022, I launched Zella Money together with the super-savvy Cait Bransgrove, licensed finance broker, finance tech guru and Post-it note aficionado, so we could help millennials like us achieve their home-ownership goals. And believe me, I know what it takes to get there . . .

Although these days I'm far wiser, I share a similar money story to many in the She's on the Money community. After taking out a credit card at university, my debts blew out over several years to an eye-watering $45,000. Back then, my key guide to finance was 'debt is bad', but I also needed serious funds to support the lifestyle I thought I was supposed to live. I really didn't understand the difference between 'good debt' and 'bad debt', so although I always met my minimum repayments (and my hair always looked fabulous), high interest rates coupled with unrestrained spending saw my debt balloon.

As a student psychologist, I knew that my bad skin breakouts were about more than just drinking too many soft drinks – my money stress was affecting my health as well as my bank balance. So I set about educating myself and giving my finances a major makeover.

It was a tough journey, but after following many of the budgeting and wealth-creation tips I now share, I was finally able to pay down my loan, swap my 'bad' debt for 'good', and get myself a degree in the process. Today, although I still have a large HECS/HELP loan (good debt!) and a mortgage (more good debt!), by relieving my personal loan burden I have been able to build several successful businesses, set up a strong investment portfolio and buy my own home – none of which I ever thought possible back when I was 24.

While many in our community share similar successes in turning their financial lives around, we receive literally thousands of posts from our followers wondering how it might *ever* be possible for them to afford property. For many millennials, it seems an unachievable goal. The world is so different from when our parents were somehow able to buy homes for less than $100,000 and service their mortgages comfortably on only one income, let alone bringing kids into the equation.

But I'm here to tell you: it *is* possible. My mortgage-broking business, Zella Money, sits down with hopeful first-time buyers every week. By carefully reviewing their personal goals, accessing available government grants and support schemes and cleverly managing their budgets, we know it *is* feasible for people of our age and stage to own their home (and still have a life).

That said, as the She's on the Money community well knows, investing in property is not the only strategy I advocate for wealth creation. Owning property is not for everyone, and even if it is the right choice for you, it must always be a considered decision made at the right time.

In this book, we'll take a big-picture view of how property sits among various investment options, consider what the property market has done over time and how that aligns with your own goals and values, and step through the pros and cons of property ownership. Following that, I'll walk you through how to go about buying property in Australia. We'll review budgets, financing and government support schemes, what to look for in property, common pitfalls to avoid, how to buy – cither through private treaty or auction, and how to set up your ownership structure properly. Then, once you have bought, how to protect your investment and increase its value over time.

It's a lot, I know. If some of that went straight over your head, don't worry. Every bit of industry-speak used to make us feel stupid and middle-aged real-estate men feel smart will be broken down and explained in real talk using clear terms that make sense.

I also know you have some serious budgeting requirements that may include Sunday brunch or once-in-a-lifetime holidays – and friend, I am all about supporting your best life, not killing it. You won't find me advocating beans on toast for the next decade just so you can afford shelter. Neither do you have to listen to the grey-haired brigade moaning about your so-called avocado life-style. If you happen to like a bit of green smoosh on your brekky toast, following these tips will show you how you *can* enjoy it, *and* your oat latte, *and* buy property too. If that's what you want.

'But Victoria, I'm single and live in a capital city and only earn $70,000 a year. You can't possibly be talking to me.'

I want to assure you that I am *absolutely* talking to you. And to those of you looking to buy as a couple, and to any post-starter-wedding peeps who may be bringing up kids on your own. We have stories from our community of people from *all* walks of life who have all managed to buy property. If this is your dream too, then the first, most important step is educating yourself around all the possible ways this could manifest (and, yes, all the potential stress it may deliver).

Let's get you looking at this with your eyes wide open and hearts hopeful. Let's talk about the best and worst that could happen. Let's take a serious look at your finances and support network and at what your future might look like if you do or don't invest in yourself. Because if there's one thing I need to make clear, it's that the best thing we can do for ourselves is secure our own financial future. Despite the gender pay gap and male–female wealth disparity, it *is* possible for us to change our financial futures by building our wealth muscles, one made-by-you protein ball (#savingshack) at a time. Sit in the driver's seat of your own life and give yourself *all* the choices. Only then can you decide if property is right for you. And friend, if it is, then strap in, because have I got some savvy tips and spicy intel coming your way.

Chapter 1

So, you want to buy property

So, you like the idea of owning property? Or you did before you started looking at your finances and listening to the daily news reports about interest-rate increases and the rising cost of living, and how millennials will never be able to afford a home ... and since the world is going to hell in a handbasket anyway, why bother?

The truth is, that yes, all the rising rates and costs do creep in, inch by painful inch, and at times of high stress, they can really start to bite. So even if you *had* once thought it possible to dream about owning your own home, now you may not really be so sure. But you don't need to give up on your property aspirations just because it seems too hard.

The first step that I always suggest on your financial journey is to analyse your personal money story – the conscious and subconscious beliefs we carry around wealth which direct our attitudes and behaviours towards money; in this case, property.

If you're interested in taking a deeper dive into your personal money story, you can find out more in Chapter 1 of my first book, *She's on the Money*. But if you're keen to find out how it plays out for you in terms of property, I suggest you stay right here. Very shortly, we'll work through some activities to get you thinking about it in detail.

Key terms

Before we get into it, I want to assure you that this book has been created with the idea of simplifying the property-buying process, not making it harder. But I'm not gonna lie, as part of the finance world, property is an acronym-heavy landscape. Learning this language – as with any language: French, Mandarin, Beautician – may be confusing at first. But trust me, the more you hear a word and see it used, the more sense it will make. Over time, you may even find yourself throwing terms like 'LMI' and 'P&I' around with loose abandon (Chapter 6 if you want to jump ahead).

As we go along, I will do my best to explain things, which includes popping Key Terms near the top of every chapter to give you a heads up, and then going into more detail on these as we progress. I'll also include a quick explainer in the moment. But if ever you find yourself being slammed with gobbledygook, there's also a handy Glossary at the back of the book, where all the terminology is listed.

KEY TERMS

comparisonitis: comparing yourself with others and finding yourself lacking or gloating, neither of which is healthy.

investor-owner: someone who owns property that they rent out for income (not to live in themselves).

Emergency Fund: a savings account holding enough money to support you for three months (housing, food, bills) if, for any reason, you can't work and/or something unexpected pops up.

financial freedom: having enough money to live securely so you can choose how to spend your time.

FOMO: fear of missing out.

gender pay gap: the real difference between what men and women are paid – typically women are paid less (for so many reasons there's not enough room to cover it all here).

Great Australian Dream: historically, the 'Great Australian Dream' was to own a quarter-acre block of land with a house on it in which to raise 2.4 children. More recently, it's come to mean owning your own home (whatever that looks like).

mortgage: another word for home loan.

owner-occupier: someone who lives in the property they own.

passive income stream: money coming in from sources other than your own direct labour. This might include things like dividends, interest, subscriptions, royalties, rent etc.

SOTM: She's on the Money – my fabulous community of millennials striving to create financial freedom.

your why: the *real* reason, often subconscious, sitting deep beneath all the obvious, superficial ones, as to why you think and behave the way you do.

Your property–money story

Okay, so are you ready to begin? I'm excited and I hope you are too.

First things first, because you know I like to get deep and it's important you do the same, at least as far as your relationship with money goes. This relationship is one of your life's most important . . . it affects your lifestyle and investment choices, including property ownership, and ultimately, your future. So understanding your attitudes and assumptions around money is essential.

Some hate the idea of having all their wealth tied up in one concrete asset, while others love it. Some investors get excited when interest rates rise – an opportunity to pick up bargains – while others faint at their mere mention. And others don't see property as particularly meaningful in either direction.

Before I start getting too deep into theory, let's get you into the property mood with this fun activity. Cue your fave music, beverage of choice and comfy set-up. BYO pen.

● ●

YOUR PROPERTY–MONEY STORY

Thinking about your property-money story, circle the statement below that best fits your ideas of being a property owner:

a) I have no idea how I'm ever going to afford property, but I'd like to. I suppose I imagine that somehow, in the future, I'll manifest a better income/partner/life to enable it.

b) I've never considered that owning property is an option for me.

c) I move around a lot and the idea of being stuck in one place, let alone owning it, is my worst nightmare.

d) I have been dreaming about owning my own property since a young age and am actively taking steps to making this dream come true.

● ●

Australian attitudes to property

Whatever you answered above, it's true and valid. But I'd like to get you thinking about where your ideas and values have come from.

In Australia, when it comes to property, we've been encouraged to believe that the 'Great Australian Dream' is owning our own home. Yet in many countries in Europe, it is entirely normal and expected that a family will rent and live in the same house for generations. Stable and secure, tenants have a say in how the place is fixed and decorated and never question paying rent for a lifetime.

Your money story is influenced by your education and upbringing. You may have grown up surrounded by a clan of powerful female property investors who modelled to you from a young age that it's entirely possible, if not expected, to own several properties in adulthood. More likely, if you look at Australia's housing statistics, you either grew up moving from house to house as renting was your family's norm, or lived in a standard family home that was paid off using a good portion of your parents' wages each month.

Australian government statistics, from 1981 to now, show that although it has fluctuated, Australian home ownership is an even split, almost 30/30/30 between those who are a) renting, b) own with mortgage, and c) own outright.[1] Nonetheless, the dream of owning your own 'castle' was the theme song of our upbringing; the typical Aussie plan for securing 'a decent life'.[2]

A lot of this was built on the idea of an Australia far removed from the society we live in today and which, it can't go without acknowledging, exists on land stolen from its original custodians. There's a lot to rectify on that front, which needs its own whole book to explore, however, we can't discuss Australian property without recognising that all this housing we're talking about sits on unceded Aboriginal land. Please bear that in mind and pay respect as you use the resources of this great country to build up your own lives and help others.

You may be wondering whether the Great Australian Dream is still a possibility, or even if it's a dream you want for yourself at all. At the end of the day, whether you invest in property or shares or simply your own education, creating financial security is about empowering you to use money as a tool to transform your life and the lives of others for the better. To start you off, I'll get you to explore your personal ideas and ambitions around property, which will help form the basis of a strategy for fulfilling those dreams, whatever they entail.

Why property is important for women

Now while we welcome any, all and no gender in our SOTM community, it is important that we talk about women when it comes to finance and property. For those who don't identify as female please stay with me as it's equally relevant to marginalised and disenfranchised groups, and as a society, affects us all.

Investing in property can be particularly important for those looking to secure their financial future and personal safety. As covered more in depth in the following chapter, these reasons can be more emotionally driven than finance-led; however, it's important to take both into account when making decisions that are right for you.

Housing affordability is a real issue for women due to several factors, including the gender pay gap (on base salary, 13.3 per cent in Australia)[3] and society's reliance on women to carry the burden of domestic and caring duties which forces them to work fewer or more flexible hours. Traditionally women-dominated industries tend to be paid less than male-dominated industries, and while things are changing, often women are still paid less for doing the same job as a man.

This data was confirmed by the Australian Bureau of Statistics (ABS) in early 2023, which found that women earn, on average, 87 cents for every dollar earned by a man, or $253.50 less per week.[3] All of these factors limit a woman's ability to save for a house deposit while stretching the time it takes, making it harder to achieve – especially when fighting against rising property prices. It also affects her ability to service a loan. On average, it takes Australian women a year longer than their male counterparts to save a deposit for a home.[4]

Even while women are starting to earn decent salaries and, in some cases, outearn men, we're still often worse off when it comes to money matters. Women are commonly kept out of the conversation when it comes to discussing finances at home, and no-one is taught about it properly in school. Quite simply, 'managing money' isn't a subject that women are encouraged to focus on. It's not that we're not smart enough; it's simply often assumed that we're not interested.

Women are also at higher risk of homelessness due to their increased vulnerability to domestic violence. Financial independence gives you agency over your life decisions and future. Being dependent on others for your financial welfare, whether another person, organisation or the government, often comes with directives on how to behave in line with the donor's principles rather than yours.

Let's turn that around! If you have dreams of owning property and no idea how on earth you're going to get there, you're not alone. If you've been trying to save for a house deposit that just seems to be getting further and further out of reach, you're not alone there either. By the time we finish this book, the goal you have for your home may look a little different from the white-picket-fence dream you were sold as a child, but it will come with the knowledge and skills to turn it into a reality.

Why property is important for your future

Speaking of futures, while retirement seems a loooong way off and most of us dream of finishing work for good one day, the harsh reality is that women often don't have enough money to support themselves in retirement. While the government enforces superannuation contributions during your employment, because women often take significant periods off work due to pregnancy, childcare and other caring and domestic duties, their superannuation at retirement is, on average, significantly less than males.[5]

Many Australians rely on selling the family home come retirement and putting these funds towards their post-salary lifestyle. If you are able to pay down a mortgage to increase your property equity (how much you, not the bank, owns) over the period of your working life, this has the potential to offer a nice buffer in retirement. In addition, if you manage to pay off your home by the time you retire, the majority of your accommodation costs will be taken care of, greatly reducing your outgoings.

Your why

First up, *before* deciding on the how, what, when and where of your own personal property journey, it's important to know what's driving your decision and the ultimate goals you're striving for – *your why*.

When the chips are down and you're eating two-minute noodles for the fifth Friday in a row so you can meet your increased mortgage repayment, you're going to need a pretty solid reason as to why you agreed to all this in the first place. Buying property is a long-term relationship that's not easy to jump out of in a hurry! (That said, we look at various ways to keep your current lifestyle, or close to it, while paying down an asset at the same time, throughout the book.)

Figuring out your why

If you come to my mortgage broking team at Zella Money, the first thing they'll ask you is: what kind of property are you looking to buy? And I'm going to let you in on a secret: they won't be satisfied with the answer, 'Oh, well, I just want to buy a house.'

They will keep prompting you . . . What kind of house? Who's going to live there – you, or is it an investment? Where is it located? Are you ready now, or making a five-year plan? Why is this so important to you? – until you both have a really clear picture.

'Honestly Victoria, I really haven't thought about it. Can you give me some ideas?'

Everyone's why will be different. Where some are purely interested in buying property to generate an income stream, others are driven by the need to provide shelter for themselves and their family. Some might be doing it alone, while others will be doing it in partnership. Some may want to run a business from home, others are looking to create a private sanctuary.

The great thing is that *all these options* are available to you. The tough thing is figuring out which ones work best for *you*. So, let's lay out a few ways to assess where you're at now and where you'd like to be at eventually.

• •

YOUR WHY

Getting to the heart of what's driving your desire to buy property is a great place to start. There will likely be several reasons, but there will usually be one main belief or motivation driving your decision. It could be the pull of having a place to call your own. Or maybe using property to create a passive income (earnings from something other than your own time and labour). For everyone, your budget will have a big influence on any financial decisions you make, and buying a house may well be the biggest financial decision you ever make.

Take some time to reflect on the question below. Dig deep and be honest with your answer.

Why is buying a property so important to you?

....

....

....

....

....

• •

The pros and cons of investing in property

Whether you are financially ready or just starting out, there is real pressure to buy property in Australia. There's a LOT to consider around property before you can make the decision to purchase, and even if you determine that buying property is definitely for you, you still want to make sure to buy the right place at the right time.

If you're a dedicated SOTM member, it's likely that you're driven by the goal of financial freedom – life supported by a passive income stream. The question is: is property the right way for you to achieve this, or are there other strategies that are better for you?

In my second book, *Investing with She's on the Money*, we look in detail at a number of investment pathways that can help build up your wealth. There is absolutely no expectation that property has to be the vehicle for this (although it can be!). Some, like *Rich Dad, Poor Dad*'s Robert Kiyosaki, suggest that 'owning your own home is not an asset' – however, this viewpoint is challenged by many, especially in regards to Australian property.[6] My thoughts are that while property can be an epic asset, your family home shouldn't be viewed as such.

As with all financial purchases and lifestyles, comparisonitis is the devil – particularly because it's so hard to really know everyone else's history or circumstances beyond what you might see from the outside. You'll know, either from your own experience or from listening to my podcast, that comparisonitis can lead us down a path paved with bad debt, so we certainly don't want to invite it in at the scale of a mortgage!

Before you agree to any property purchase, I really encourage you to think about what it is you're committing to and why, run the numbers several times, and follow the book's activities to test your saving and repayment thresholds before you sign on the dotted line. Remember: when it comes to figuring out the best way to build YOUR future wealth, you're truly running your own race!

Let's briefly consider some of the pros and cons of investing in property. We'll look at many of these in more detail later, but just to get your brain juices flowing, here are some considerations unique to property investing.

Ten reasons why . . .

Pros of investing in property

1. You meet the human need for shelter.
2. It's a place to call your own.
3. You can use and enjoy it while you're paying it off (the ultimate buy now, pay later!).
4. Compared with some investments, it's reasonably straightforward to understand.
5. Median property values, historically, have grown over time.
6. It's typically a stable investment over the medium-to-long term.
7. It can generate income and/or reduce the costs of running a business.
8. It offers the potential to reduce your tax (negative gearing).
9. It can create access to funding when used as a security (rather than cash).
10. You can have a direct impact on improving its value (unlike buying shares in a company).

Cons of investing in property

1. It can be really, really expensive.
2. It may keep you in debt for a long time.
3. It's difficult to predict interest rates, which can impact your standard of living.
4. You may not be able to afford the house of your dreams, so find yourself paying off something you don't 'really' love (unless we change your property mindset – more on that to come!).
5. It's hard to cash in quickly (what investors call an 'illiquid asset' – unlike cash, which is 'liquid' and immediately available).
6. Holding onto a property costs money in ongoing maintenance, fees (rates, body corporate) and perhaps in lost or below-market rental income, among other things.

7. Property is not a 'set-and-forget' investment; it requires ongoing care and maintenance.
8. Property involves many moving parts and people, which can bring potential issues.
9. Capital growth is not guaranteed – despite what people like to say, the property market does not uniformly rise in every area, every seven years.
10. It can be risky if you invest in areas slow to develop, or you are trying to make fast money using a 'flip' strategy during times when the market drops.

Your property beliefs, values and goals

Let's look a little more closely at your personal property beliefs, goals and values. You may find that working through the prompts below will get you to reconsider your initial 'why'. That's good! It means you've really started thinking more deeply about what property means for you and how it might fit into and impact your life.

To figure out what makes you tick and why you're thinking about committing to the biggest expense of your lifetime, let's walk through a series of questions together. Either write your notes in the spaces below, or if you're a dedicated diarist, grab a notebook and pen (if you're like me, a shiny new one especially for all your property dreams, goals and strategies) – and let's begin!

What are your main reasons for buying property?

Seriously, have you really sat down and thought about this – I mean, properly? A lot of people we talk to at Zella and She's on the Money think they want to 'get into property' without ever having spent the time to consider why. Is owning real estate *really* that big on your list of priorities or is it just something you've been conditioned to believe is important?

As we've talked about, we grew up being fed the Great Australian Dream. But take a look around, friend – is that *your* dream? Does it chime with who you want to be? Australia has thankfully become far more open and inclusive in recent years. People live in all sorts of families and practise wildly different lifestyles. The desire to follow 'the norm' is losing its grip, if there's even a 'norm' at all.

So, before you decide to commit to a significant cash drop, be sure you know why you're doing it. All reasons are equally valid, so this is just about getting clear on *your* reason.

• •

WHY ARE YOU THINKING OF BUYING PROPERTY?

- For a place to call your own?
- To live in just for now?
- To live in well into the future?
- As a wealth-creating strategy (investor)?
- As your retirement plan (for its long-term growth)?
- Because you're sick of landlords and want a say in the place?
- Because you're terrified of becoming homeless?
- Because your parents told you it was a good idea?
- Actually, come to think of it, no thanks, or at least, not right now.

....

....

....

....

....

• •

The financial commitment of a property loan

If you are seriously thinking about investing in property, do you understand what that means for your finances? We have gone through several reasons why owning property may be a particularly valuable investment for women, but that doesn't necessarily apply to *all* women, and certainly not all people.

Taking on home ownership is a serious financial commitment. Not only must you save up for a deposit, you must first establish yourself as a positive loan risk for the bank to take on. That could mean extra effort to create an additional savings account, work to clear your existing personal loans, reducing or eliminating your credit card debts and possibly taking on extra work or employment.

ARE YOU READY TO TAKE ON A PROPERTY LOAN?

- Have you got it in you right now?
- And even if you *can* do it for a sprint, are you sure you can sustain it for the long term, remembering that a standard mortgage repayment term is 30 years?
- What savings do you already have and how much more might you need for a deposit?
- How much can/are you willing to direct towards paying a home loan for the next 30 years or so?
- Are you comfortable with the restrictions this might have on your lifestyle?
- List out some things you might have to forfeit if you were paying down a loan. How does this make you feel?

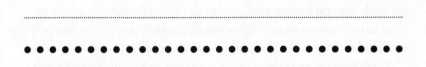

··

··

··

●●●●●●●●●●●●●●●●●●●●●●●●●●●●●●●●●●●●

The reality of managing a long-term loan

Now, I don't want to get all doom-and-gloomy, but you have to consider how you might be able to keep paying your mortgage if the worst happened. (We'll look more deeply at this in Chapter 7, so no need to get teary, but it's definitely worth thinking about.)

During Covid, the government introduced wage support, banks offered moratoriums on repayments and many landlords went over and above to keep their tenants housed, but it won't always be 'all in together' when shit hits the fan.

If you already had a home loan and got so severely injured yesterday that you couldn't work today, what then? Hopefully, after reading this book, you'll have got yourself some reliable insurances, and SOTM-smart savers will already have a decent Emergency Fund, which they will increase when they become homeowners. But these plans don't magically appear, and neither do the funds to support them. Make this conversation part of your planning.

●●●●●●●●●●●●●●●●●●●●●●●●●●●●●●●●●●●●

ARE YOU PREPARED TO MANAGE A LONG-TERM LOAN?

- Since 1990 to now, mortgage interest rates have ranged between 2.14 and 15.5 per cent. Could you manage this?
- If so, how – what plans would you put in place?

- What about if you couldn't work for whatever reason – can you afford insurance that would cover you in this event (and/or other support plans)?
- Who might be there for you? Where might you turn?
- Is this a realistic plan for the short and long term?

....

....

....

....

....

● ●

The responsibilities of owning property

Owning a property might sound like a dream come true, but even once you've saved that deposit, bought the place and furnished it with your snazzy-but-affordable knick-knacks, it's no time to kick back and lie like a lady lizard drinking in the sun. Owning a property comes not only at an ongoing financial cost, but a social and emotional one too.

If you bought your place to live in, it's almost a guarantee that something (many things) had to give. Maybe you now have a 90-minute one-way commute, maybe you need to spend every second Sunday mowing the lawns because the landlord doesn't cover it anymore. Maybe you had to forfeit two months of Sunday brunches because your hot-water system blew up the day after you moved in.

If you get bored with the place, or itchy for a new lifestyle (one-year hiatus in Hawaii, anyone?), changing things up becomes far more difficult as a homeowner. As a renter, you simply give notice and move on with your life. If the property's yours, it's yours to deal with too. That's not to say you can't rent it out, or even sell it – but both these are more hassle than giving two weeks' notice.

Then there's being a landlord. If you're an investor-owner, you may not have sacrificed your walk-to-work proximity, but if you have tenants, you may be required to fix any issue they have with the house or appliances, quick-smart. If the breakdown happens over a weekend and is considered a health risk, hello, emergency call-out fee!

Whatever compromises you talked yourself into when you bought the place, triple them. More things go wrong than you will have ever thought of. Soon enough, you'll have listened to every single one of my podcasts and that commute won't seem so shiny anymore. That lovely lawn that you imagined lying on, reading SOTM book after SOTM book, has now become your worst nightmare. Those dream tenants who promised to lovingly tend your place? Gremlins.

The trouble with property is that it's a long-term commitment. You will probably have times when you get more sick of it than it could ever get of you. Worse still, *unlike* an annoying ex-boyfriend or bad haircut, you can't just ignore your house and its problems when you're over it. No matter what, those pesky bills will keep showing up and the bank will keep drawing down its fee. When you sign up for a home loan, you're committing to possibly the longest relationship you'll ever have.

There are plenty of lifestyle limitations that come with owning property beyond just the mortgage repayments. That's not to say it won't be worth it overall, but now's the time to have a good, hard think about whether you're ready to give up your current lifestyle to support your dream and Future You.

ARE YOU READY TO BE A RESPONSIBLE PROPERTY OWNER?

- Is 'making a home' something that interests you?
- To what degree – are floofy cushions enough, or do you dream of floorplans and paint colours and exactly which oven you'd like in your kitchen?
- What about if these break down? If the windows start leaking, or the gas heating stops working, or your front door won't shut properly?
- Have you got the time, inclination and budget to deal directly with builders and handymen to keep the place upright and secure?
- Are you ready to settle into living in a place for, possibly, the next 30 years (or, at least seven, to make it worthwhile)?

....

....

....

....

....

The responsibilities of being a landlord

There's a lot of chat around about the terrors of landlords, so let's tame that beast, shall we? If you're thinking about owning property, chances are you may one day become a landlord yourself, either by choice or necessity.

If you've been a renter yourself, or even if you've just watched the news lately, it's clear that while some landlords are greedy monsters, the majority are regular folk who got lucky and/or worked hard to get a foot into property investment. These people are now doing their best to look after their own finances and the people who live in the home they provide.

Everyone has a choice in this world: to be a dick, or not to be a dick. So you can be a landlord, just don't be a landlord dick. The best way to do that is to know and fulfil your responsibilities under the law, and ideally go beyond those to ensure your tenants are comfortable. You don't have to buy them super-large fluffy beanbags or send a weekly grocer's box, but a nice welcome note and the invitation to get in touch should they need anything goes a long way to making them feel human. If you decide to employ a property manager, make sure to choose an ethical one who will do right by you and by your tenants.

Also – and most importantly – make sure you have allocated enough funds to looking after the joint. As a landlord, you may have to fix things straight away, even if it's something you might live with if it were your own home. So, make sure you have the cash to service your property. You might need a redraw facility on your property loan, or consider getting landlord's insurance to help cover unexpected costs. Being financially responsible as an investor-owner will take the emotion out of it and help ensure that both you and your tenants are looked after in the long run.

• •

ARE YOU READY TO BE A RESPONSIBLE LANDLORD?

- If you're a landlord, you must attend to issues straight away. Do you have the time, inclination and budget to make repairs?
- If not, are you willing to pay and work with a managing agent to do so?

- Does your budget stretch to covering rental vacancies, tenant and/or building damages, special levies and other unexpected costs?
- Are you willing to sacrifice your own lifestyle, if needed, to ensure your tenants and property are looked after?

● ●

The ethical implications of owning property

Further to the landlord dilemma, people are becoming increasingly aware of the social impact of their decisions. Investors call this 'value investing', and in recognition of this, many trading platforms allow you the option to invest only in funds or companies that align with your personal values.

A similar thought process can apply in property. The choice you make in materials to renovate or fix your home, what power you use for your heating and cooking and even what kind of plants you grow, all affect the environment. The impact of one person owning several houses when it's well acknowledged that thousands of people around Australia sleep rough every night and that our property's sit on unceded Aboriginal land, can give some people the ick.

There are many ways, large and small, to help rebalance such disparity. You might consider investing in social housing or land reclamation projects, or contributing some of your income to supporting marginalised groups. For example, Pay The Rent is a grassroots Aboriginal initiative encouraging Australians to pay a small percentage of their income as rent for living on unceded lands. There are several organisations that provide shelter to vulnerable women who welcome donations, both in time and money.

As with any philanthropy, you can give in-kind support, fundraise or myriad other initiatives that help to counterbalance the impact you have on the planet. It's up to you how creative you want to get. I'd love to hear your ideas, so be sure you let us know by commenting on our Insta or via our She's on the Money website. Together, we can make all the difference.

• •

WHAT ARE YOUR ETHICS
AROUND PROPERTY OWNERSHIP?

- As with any investment or lifestyle, there are ethical implications to your decision and ways to mitigate against the negative impacts. Have you considered investing in schemes or activities that can work to building housing affordability?
- Can you list a few options?
- How about ensuring your building is environmentally sustainable?
- What are some things you could implement to ensure this?

....

....

....

• •

Your *real* why

It's easy to see why and how we inherit beliefs from society and others around us. If we're not actively reflecting on our own personal reasons and beliefs around life, money and what's important to us, we can be swayed by others' stories, views and fears – many of which may well have been developed decades ago against very different circumstances. Not to mention that you, my pretty butterfly, are the *only you* on this planet, and so what you think, feel and ultimately do should be individual to you.

● ●

YOUR *REAL* WHY BUYING A HOUSE IS SO IMPORTANT TO YOU . . .

Working through this chapter, you have reviewed your property-money beliefs, and thought more about which of these are true to *your story* and those you may have inherited from others. Reflecting on these, what is now true for you?

....

....

....

● ●

RUBY, 32 – NZ/NSW

My partner and I are from New Zealand. After years of saving for a house, we became demoralised by increasing prices and the hundreds of people at open homes where we were looking to buy in Wellington. After the Covid borders opened, we decided to give up on our NZ property dream, move to Sydney and chuck our money into shares, bonds and a couple of start-up businesses. We're so *thankful not to have the $1 million of debt and rising interest costs to think about if we had bought a house. We now have no desire to buy property and I can't see that changing in the next five to ten years.*

MICHANA, 30 – VIC

I moved to Australia when I was 19 and, since then, have dreamt of owning my own house instead of paying someone else's mortgage. We started saving for a loan deposit in 2015, when I was earning just $43,000 a year and my husband was earning $25 an hour as a casual. As we didn't have much knowledge of the property market, our mortgage broker was invaluable, guiding us from the start of the process until the end – he's now a family friend. We secured a mortgage on incomes of $54,000 and $50,000, respectively. We've been in our house for a bit over four years and now have enough equity to buy an investment house. The market is scarier than it looked when we purchased the first time, but my knowledge keeps growing and I know I'll never look back.

● ● ● ● ● ●

TAKE NOTE

Buying property is a big decision and a serious commitment – possibly the longest relationship you'll have in your life! – so, not one to take on lightly.

....

Property comes with pros and cons and is not the only pathway towards building future wealth.

....

Dig deep to identify the true reason you want to buy property (if you still do!) and use that to guide you from here.

....

Chapter 2

The big-picture view

Friend, I'm not going to lie: the current stage of the property-market cycle is pinching. *A lot.* I recently managed to buy my first house, so I feel all that interest-rate and high-inflation pain too. Believe me!

Weighing up all the factors, I chose not to fix my low-interest mortgage rate back when the rates were quite low. While I don't love paying a much higher interest rate than what I started on, I also know it's just part of the cycle. One aimed at trying to bring the cost of living back down and our wages' buying power back up. As a former financial adviser, I'm onboard with it. (Doesn't mean it doesn't sting, though.)

While many things have changed since our parents and grand-parents were buying houses, the economic cycle, including inflation, has not – and who knows if it ever will. What *has* changed, though, is the relative buying power of our income compared to the cost of housing . . . and this is what's at the heart of all the bad press.

Since I always say that education is your way out of a bad situation, in this chapter we'll take a proper look at all these terms – inflation, interest rates, the market – so you can be fully informed about the property-buying journey and its potential impacts. Interest-rate fluctuations are part and parcel of the fun journey of property ownership – the ride you sign up for if you choose to jump onboard this particular train – so let's find out more.

KEY TERMS

borrowing capacity: how much a bank is willing to lend you, based on your income and expenses.

RBA (the): the Reserve Bank of Australia – our central bank – maintains a healthy financial system, in part, by setting the cash rate and providing liquidity to financial institutions.

cash rate: the RBA sets the base (wholesale) lending rate in Australia, otherwise called the cash rate, to help keep the economy stable.

global financial crisis (GFC): the period of extreme stress in global financial markets and banking systems between mid 2007 and early 2009, initiated by a downturn in the US housing market.

inflation: the increase, over time, of the cost of goods and services. If wages don't keep up with price increases, your buying power is reduced.

interest rates: the fee charged to borrow money, usually a percentage of the initial loan amount (principal).

mortgage affordability: how much of a person's income is being directed to pay their mortgage – industry guidelines suggest it should be no more than 30 per cent.

> **principal:** the initial amount borrowed when establishing a loan.

The long view on the Australian property market

There's been a lot of talk in 2023 of the 'cost-of-living crisis' and 'rapidly rising interest rates' and at the time of writing, experts are stating that mortgage affordability appears, quite frankly, unaffordable. So I reckon it's quite fair to wonder why anyone in their right mind would ever consider buying property. Even if they *could* possibly afford it.

If we look at the long-term view of property in Australia – say the last 30 years, from 1990 to 2020 – property prices in most capital cities have steadily risen. Even in the last ten years or so, as the following graph shows, while housing prices have had some short-term declines, ultimately, they recovered then increased again.

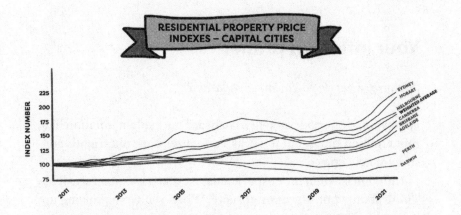

Combined House and Attached Dwellings Price Indexes
(Source: ABS[7])

This will not necessarily forever be the case, with certain economists suggesting that tightening mortgage affordability and lending rates will ultimately force house prices to come down. If you're not yet in the property market, that would be a dream scenario. Trouble is, apart from short-term periods, we haven't seen this play out. So, to now, people who've chosen to wait for this to happen have found themselves priced out of an ever-increasing market.

'Victoria, why does this keep happening? Surely something has to help make housing more affordable?'

The thing is, there are so many factors at play, and both sides of the equation to consider. Those already in the housing market pray that prices won't plummet, as this could see their life savings disappear down the drain. Those yet to buy are desperate for house prices to stop rising.

The government has a few, limited levers they can and do use to help; interest rates being one, buyers' grants and schemes another. Let's take a closer look.

Your inflation primer

'Victoria, what do you mean by inflation?'

Followers of our podcast will have heard me explain inflation like this a million times, but it works, so bear with me old friends and strap in new ones . . .

Inflation is when the cost of goods rises, so our dollar buys less. Think about your Maccas soft serve. When you were growing up it cost like, 30 (maybe 50) cents, right? For me and my sister, it was our after-swimming-lesson treat, and one I was pretty keen on. Fast-forward to today and sometimes, after a summer swim,

I still love one. But these days, the exact same Maccas soft serve is going to cost me anywhere from 85 cents to $1. Yes, folks, a whole shiny dollar for exactly the same swirl of creamy vanilla goodness in the same plain cone.

Nothing about a Maccas soft serve has changed. Except for the price. And it's not because the golden arches are greedy (actually, they make a point of making low-budget meals affordable for the whole family) . . . No, the reason my soft serve now costs me $1 is because our money today is worth less than when we were kids.

SPOT THE DIFFERENCE

2003
$0.30

2023
$1.00

'Victoria, I earn three times the salary my dad started on. What do you mean my money is worth less?'

Right there, is part of the answer. You earn more, but can buy fewer things (housing being one of them). Since your dad's first job, the cost of making things has increased. For Maccas, the cost of staff, the cost of rent and the cost of ingredients to make the soft serve have all risen. For them to make and serve you a cone, it costs them a whole lot more. In turn, they have to charge *you* a lot more, just to cover their costs. Everyone's playing a big-ole game of kiss-chasies.

Now, in the grand scheme of things, a steady rise in inflation (the cost of goods and services) is a good thing. It's the sign of a healthy, growing economy and, as with any healthy growing thing, that means productivity. For plants, that means leaves (and, if you're lucky, some juicy tomatoes) and for the economy, that means more jobs. More jobs means more tax income for the government, which ideally means more support for us by way of hospitals, schools, roads and the like.

The problem is when it all runs away too fast. (Which isn't a problem I've ever encountered, personally, because running? Ugh, no thanks.) When inflation runs hot, the cost of living rises too fast for our wages to keep up. Not only do things cost more, but our buying power is reduced.

The normal rate of growth as measured by inflation is happiest around 2 to 3 per cent. So, when it starts rising too much (like in mid-2023, to 7.1 per cent), that's why the RBA, Australia's central bank, hikes interest rates. They do so in the hope it will stop people spending so much. And in turn, they hope that this will put a brake on the rapid rise in the cost of goods and services.

You see, if people are not buying quite so many hot-girl hand-bags, then the manufacturers will have to make fewer of them. It's the old supply-and-demand equation – if buyers aren't buying, then demand slows, which hopefully cools the cycle. Kinda the reverse of 'mo' money, mo' problems' – or that's the plan, anyway. The RBA hopes to reverse the problem of runaway inflation by influencing us to splash less cash.

A quick look at interest rates

So, now that we're all up to speed on inflation, what has that got to do with property? For a start, interest rates, which is where this whole chat began.

'Hey, Victoria, talk to me about interest rates.'

Interest rates are the fee a lender charges a borrower for loaning them money – usually, a percentage of the principal (the amount loaned). In Australia, our central bank, the RBA, sets the whole-sale rate (the 'cash rate') as a way to manage credit growth. Adjusting interest rates is the biggest lever the RBA has available to keep inflation at its targeted 2 to 3 per cent. If the RBA raises the cash rate, the banks that lend consumers money must, in turn, pass those rate rises on – somewhere between 1 to 3 per cent variation on the rate the RBA has set. This is not so they can make more money, but simply to keep operating at the same profit margin.

Although it might not feel like it, especially to those paying off a hefty mortgage, this ultimately benefits us all. A steadily growing economy is a healthy economy. It helps the government afford to continue supplying central support services – such as security, health, telecommunications, grants and funds – some of which, like the various schemes to help first homeowners buy property, we'll cover off in this book.

That said, when we're coming off the back of several years of historically super low interest rates – down in the 1 to 2 per cent range – any rise in rates will hit mortgage holders' back pockets.

And that can be a heavy burden to bear if you haven't factored it in. From May 2022 to June 2023, the cash rate has gone from 0.1 per cent to 4.1 per cent, bringing the cost-to-consumer rate for a variable home loan to roughly 5.5 per cent.

This is partly why investing in property can be such a big ask. First, of course, it's the price – it's not like we're buying an ice-cream (or even a whole box of them!), right? We're talking hundreds of thousands of dollars. But also, it's the unknowns and the longevity. I can't even commit to a single pair of trainers for the next six months, but when you sign up to own property, the bank generally writes you a loan with a 30-year repayment term. That's a long time, and a lot of interest-rate rollercoasters to ride along the way.

On the plus side, like any long-term investment, the longer you hold, the smoother those bumps are likely to become. As I often like to say, 'When in doubt, zoom out.' If we look at the 12-month period we're in at the time of writing, yes, the buying power of our wages against the cost of property is unsustainable. Unless you have been given a 7 per cent (or more) pay rise this year in line with inflation, then your money is actually buying you less.

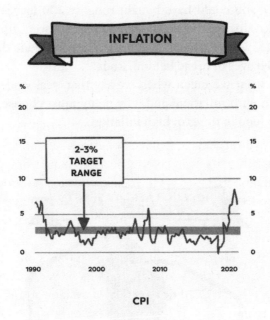

When in doubt, zoom out
(Source: RBA[8])

How inflation affects real wages

Let's say, last year you earned $70,000, which, after tax, leaves you around $55,000 – roughly $1,000 a week – to support yourself. This year, if you were lucky, you got a pay increase in line with 'normal' inflation (2.8 per cent), so your salary rose to nearly $72,000 (after tax, $56,693) or about $30 extra a week.

But at the same time, while last year your favourite loaf of bread cost $5, this year, the exact same loaf of bread costs $7.50 – a total increase of 50 per cent. But your salary's only risen 2.8 per cent, leaving you a whopping *47.2 per cent behind.*

Or, to look at it another way . . . Last year, if the only thing you purchased with your weekly salary was bread (no lattes for you, my friend), you could have bought roughly 200 loaves of bread each week. This year, even though your wage went up, you can only buy 145 loaves a week. Your real wage has gone down, and you are 55 loaves of bread behind. Rude!

That is what we mean when we say that 'real wages are not keeping up with inflation' and why many must choose between heating or food in times of high inflation.

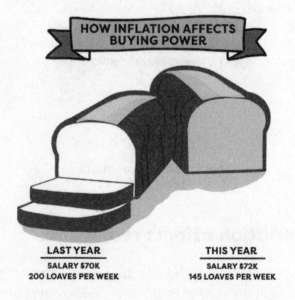

HOW INFLATION AFFECTS BUYING POWER

LAST YEAR
SALARY $70K
200 LOAVES PER WEEK

THIS YEAR
SALARY $72K
145 LOAVES PER WEEK

YOU ARE *DOWN* 55 LOAVES OF BREAD. HUNGRY MUCH?

And property, too

Obviously, like any other product, the rising cost of money affects property prices. It forces interest rates to rise and also forces the cost of everything – including builders and building materials – to go up as well. This ultimately affects the price of construction, which eventually forces property prices up across the board. Yes, even that decrepit rundown shack at the end of the street that hasn't seen a tradesman in 20 years, because, as I also often like to observe, 'a rising tide lifts all ships'.

In May 2023, AMP Capital's chief economist, Shane Oliver, reported that spending power for the average income earner was down nearly 30 per cent.[9] This is why, even though your boomer parents/uncle/neighbour keeps harping on about the extreme interest rates they had to pay back in the 90s and the devastating effects of the 2008 global economic crisis, today's mortgage affordability (how much of your after-tax income is directed towards paying your home loan) is just as bad – if not worse – if we take into account several additional impacts we'll look at below.

So, no, you are not imagining it. Looking to buy a house in today's conditions is a very real challenge. But as with every financial decision, I want you to be educated and empowered to make your own choices. Read on to learn exactly what kind of game you might be choosing to enter into.

The real price of housing and the Australian property market

The gap between the price of housing and real wages is about the worst it's ever been. Back in January 1990, when the Australian cash rate hit an all-time high of 17.5 per cent (I know, shocking, right?), mortgage affordability was its worst on record, requiring 47.1 per cent of income.

And we're almost there again.

The Real Estate Institute of Australia (REIA) Affordability Report, March 2023, showed that the proportion of income required to meet the average loan repayment in the country increased to 44.9 per cent over the March 2023 quarter, the highest since September 2008 (at the tail-end of the GFC).[10] For reference, the industry recommendation is that no more than 30 per cent of your salary should be going towards housing.[11]

'Seriously Victoria, I don't get it. Back then, the cash rate was 17.5 per cent, today it's around 4 per cent. So why is our mortgage affordability just as bad?'

Excellent question! Between May 2022 and June 2023, Australia experienced 12 (yes, 12!) interest-rate rises in quick succession. And although, as I said earlier, all property investors *should* expect fluctuations in rates over the lifetime of their loans (and savings, too, if you're a clever SOTM chickadee), this was *not* what the Reserve Bank's governor, Philip Lowe, announced in December 2021:

> **The Board will not increase the cash rate** until actual inflation is sustainably within the 2 to 3 per cent target range.[12] (My emphasis.)

The RBA's about-face caught many people unawares. This decision has pushed the average homebuyer's budget back much faster than property prices have fallen. And while over the long term this should help stabilise the economy, in the short term, the gap between the cost of a standard home and the amount an average Australian can borrow has *more than doubled*, with many economists predicting that this is likely to worsen as interest rates climb to an 11-year high.[13]

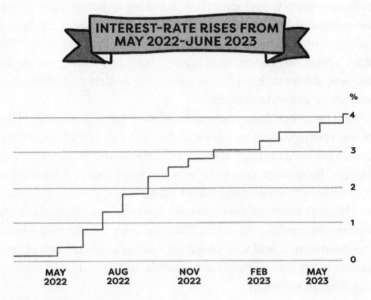

The hope here, which some economists agree with, is that all this pressure might slow the demand for housing and eventually put downward pressure on housing costs. To now, that doesn't appear to be the case. Buyer demand remains high, continuing to drive prices up.

And while this can be a great thing if you're looking to cash in your property assets, it's most definitely NOT ideal if you're wanting to get into the market with 30 per cent less borrowing capacity than what you were offered a year ago. Especially when supply remains low.

'Hang on, Victoria, if demand is so strong, then why do we have a supply issue?'

You're right to ask – I mean, shouldn't all the demand be spurring efforts to supply more property to the market? Well, while low interest rates helped drive property prices up, the Australian Investors Association (AIA) also points to other factors that are reducing supply, including low building approvals, inefficient planning and low vacancy rates, alongside increased net migration and high employment which are increasing demand.[14] The RBA agrees, suggesting that limited land availability and development approvals have forced inner-city Sydney and Melbourne apartment prices to skyrocket.[15]

And then there's our old mate, inflation (again). Another effect of unexpected, rapid increases in the cash rate is that many businesses get caught short. If the cost of goods and services goes up quickly, businesses that have sold to customers at a fixed price may find themselves strapped for cash.

This isn't usually a problem with lower-priced retail, but it can become a huge issue in the building industry when a home-build has been costed and sold based on a set of expected prices, and suddenly the cost of building materials, trades and finance virtually doubles overnight.

In these scenarios, the agreed fixed quotes (a regular thing in building) are not high enough to cover the new cost of supply. This has recently forced many building companies to go under, 'in what is becoming an increasingly common scenario in Australia's building sector', with AIA reporting that 'at least 20 construction companies in Australia folded in 2022' as 'rising labour costs, extreme weather, global supply chain issues and materials shortages have hit them hard'.[16]

Naturally, all these factors impact supply.

'But Victoria, you just said the average Aussie can borrow less, so where is the demand coming from?'

In May 2023, the *Sydney Morning Herald* reported that industry experts suggest that strong migration is partly responsible for maintaining demand. Barrenjoey's chief economist also pointed to 'gains . . . largely being led by the more affluent upper end of the market'. And in the same article, perhaps more interestingly, and what may explain just why housing affordability seems so far off for us compared to our parents' day, is what the CBA's chief economist called, 'a significant change from the way our parents paid down their mortgages . . . Affordability has gotten worse . . . someone on the average income now can't buy as good a dwelling as 20 years ago . . . [But there's also been] a structural change in the number of people working, most [households now] have a dual income.'[17]

In effect, if you are a single person looking to buy a home, you must now compete with the buying power of two incomes, whereas, back in the day, there was usually only ever one income on the table, even if a couple was buying. This makes it doubly hard for solo-salary mortgage wannabes, like many of us in the SOTM community.

There appears no way around it – with supply remaining tight, this will continue to push up demand. And when strong buyer demand and low supply combine, this puts upwards pressure on property prices.

What's a millennial to do?

With all this said, it pays to remember that no-one – not even the experts – can ever guarantee what will actually play out in the future. Case in point, this graph the RBA modelled to determine the effect of a global recession on Australia, indicating three possible outcomes of the effect of adjusting the cash rate on Australian house prices: 1) Based on the OIS (overnight index swap) implied cash rate, 2) Based on the ME (market economists') expected path, and 3) BASE – the average of the two.[18]

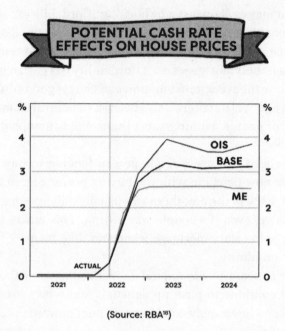

(Source: RBA[18])

So why bother with property at all?

That graph is only forecasting the next couple of years, not the long-term view. Over the long haul, property has historically been an asset that increases in value.[19] So if you can somehow afford to get in and buy your own property, it may be a worthwhile investment.

However, as my SOTM community knows, at the end of the day, my main goal is simply to help millennials like us get ahead financially. I'm not advocating that you should get into property, but rather, looking to make you fully aware of your options, so you can make investment choices that are right for you.

My previous books (particularly my second, *Investing with She's on the Money*) are rich with strategies for wealth creation through other options that allow you to begin investing, starting with just a dollar – a far cry from the tens of thousands you need for a house deposit. And before that, if you're right at the beginning of your money journey, perhaps book one, *She's on the Money*, which is full of great budgeting and money-management tips, may be the place to start.

But if you're still here, I assume you're keen on looking at property. And you're not alone. There are many good reasons that property is so appealing, but the biggest one may be that, at the end of the day, it is the only investment that you can live in. As old mate Maslow's Hierarchy of Needs model illustrates, shelter (aka, a home) sits on the foundational level of the most important things we humans need to keep us safe and happy.

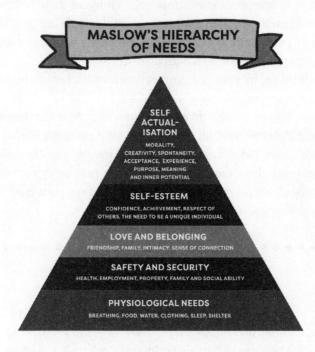

MASLOW'S HIERARCHY OF NEEDS

SELF ACTUAL-ISATION
MORALITY, CREATIVITY, SPONTANEITY, ACCEPTANCE, EXPERIENCE, PURPOSE, MEANING AND INNER POTENTIAL

SELF-ESTEEM
CONFIDENCE, ACHIEVEMENT, RESPECT OF OTHERS, THE NEED TO BE A UNIQUE INDIVIDUAL

LOVE AND BELONGING
FRIENDSHIP, FAMILY, INTIMACY, SENSE OF CONNECTION

SAFETY AND SECURITY
HEALTH, EMPLOYMENT, PROPERTY, FAMILY AND SOCIAL ABILITY

PHYSIOLOGICAL NEEDS
BREATHING, FOOD, WATER, CLOTHING, SLEEP, SHELTER

Maslow's model is a way of representing what we need to live our best lives. Needs placed lower in the hierarchy must be satisfied before individuals can attend to higher needs. He describes 'shelter' as being essential for basic survival (hard yes from me). Anyone who's watched the TV series *Alone Australia* will see that shelter is a contestant's top priority. Perhaps more interesting is that the longer we go without a basic human necessity, the more motivated we are to get it. Which means that having a place to call home is hardwired to be front of mind. As is security.

And that's why, although renting is one strategy for shelter, for some people, it may not fulfil all their essential needs. As we're all too aware, while renting may give you a place to live, it's not necessarily 'secure'. In Australia, at least, tenants have limited rights or protections, which can leave them quite vulnerable to the changing economic conditions and whims of their landlords. The same situation applies for any dependants living in a home they don't personally own. As such, for many, working towards home ownership becomes a high priority.

What's more, investing in property feels different to buying a share in a company because it's tangible (we can see it, touch it, even taste it if you want – do not recommend!). More to the point, it is something we can all understand. We get a roof over our heads while we pay off our loan and our investment (hopefully) grows in value. Fascinatingly (at least for a psychology grad like me), studies have shown that the decision to own your home can positively affect your mental wellbeing.[20]

• •

YOUR VALUES

Thinking about your own life and values, what tends to bring you the most comfort and happiness? Maybe it's being surrounded by a supportive network of family and friends. Perhaps it's challenging yourself to move beyond your comfort zone. For some, a good life might look like lots of loosely planned travel and adventure; for others, it might be a set routine that includes plenty of fun time, so long as it's scheduled and works with the rest of your life.

Thinking about these things may help you define whether your preference is to own a property for your own comfort or to build wealth, and how much you may or may not be willing to sacrifice to do either. There are loads of 'values' exercises floating around the internet, but to get you started, mark where on these sliding scales you feel most happy and pushed in the direction of your best life.

staying home	going out
fixed routines	total spontaneity
tight-knit support	complete independence
relaxation	busy schedule
travel local	destination unknown
homebase	no fixed address
familiarity	novelty
eating in	eating out
spend money for fun	invest for my future
safer blue-chip investments	riskier, high-growth stocks
host get-togethers	be a random guest
collectibles queen	minimalism is me
security	freedom

The real cost for women

With all we've learned so far about the current economic climate, there's no denying that for those yet to break into the housing market, especially on a single income, the opportunity appears pretty far out of reach. I mean, when we can hardly afford to eat, how on earth can we afford to allocate any extra percentage of our salary (let alone nearly 50 per cent!)[21] to paying off a loan we're not even sure we want?

The real question, though, is can you afford NOT to? My mission with everything I do at She's on the Money is to help put people in the driver's seat of their finances. I stress how important it is to be financially independent, especially because when we look at the stats in Australia, millennial women have some catching up to do.

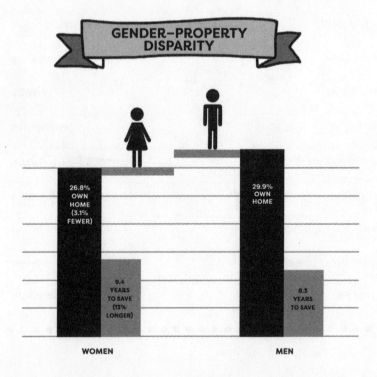

GENDER–PROPERTY DISPARITY

26.8% OWN HOME (3.1% FEWER)

9.4 YEARS TO SAVE (13% LONGER)

29.9% OWN HOME

8.3 YEARS TO SAVE

WOMEN

MEN

Research from CoreLogic tells us that in 2023, 26.8 per cent of Aussie women own a home, compared with 29.9 per cent of men. Since, in general, houses go up in value over time, that means over 3 per cent of women are potentially missing out on a decent slice of wealth and financial security. As discussed in Chapter 1, the gender pay gap seriously impacts a woman's ability to pull together a deposit, with CoreLogic reporting that women need 9.4 years to save for a 20 per cent deposit, compared to men who need 8.3 years.[22]

It is not just the short- and medium-term picture we should think about, either. Research from the Australian Institute's Centre for Future Work found that women in Australia earn $1 million dollars less over their lifetimes than men (read that again – sickening, right?) and retire with $136,000 less in superannuation.[23] Many Australian households rely on accessing the equity in their family home to bulk out their retirement savings, which is why purchasing your first home could make a real difference to your comfort and security later in life.

Quite simply, it could mean having a place to live. ABC News reported that census night 2016 counted 2,186 homeless women – a rise of 48 per cent from the previous record. That for women aged 65 to 74, the increase was 78 per cent. And that the Housing for the Aged Action Group (HAAG) estimated that the true number of women aged 55 and over at risk of homelessness was closer to 240,000 around the country, with many couch-surfing or living in cars to avoid the shame of admitting their real circumstances.[24]

At the end of the day, the reason I am so committed to empowering women to gain financial freedom is to give us choice and the opportunity to safeguard our futures. We all want to assume our lives and our choice in partners will work out for the best. However, the sobering stats are that one in six women have experienced physical and/or sexual violence, one in four have experienced emotional abuse and one in five have experienced sexual violence.[25] As women, we can't downplay the importance of being able to get out of a harmful situation.

Even the most loving and supportive relationships can be hit by unexpected health and work hardships. We just don't know what's around the corner, so the sooner we start securing our financial future, the better. Owning property can be just one tool to help us do that, as are the many approaches to financial management and wealth creation we talk about in the She's on the Money community.

Okay, my friend! That was some sobering reading, but I'm guessing you're still keen to learn how to achieve owning property for yourself. So whether you're ready now or it's a so-far-off-on-the-horizon-I-can-barely-see-it goal, then let's get into it.

Your investment options

Investing in property has been a cultural stronghold of the Australian investment psyche. Historically, property prices have generally risen in value over time. But, despite what the renovation-makeover TV shows may suggest, property is usually not a 'quick-win' opportunity. There are significant upfront costs plus ongoing costs and the unknown of interest rate variations to deal with along the way. Before you invest in property, it is important you consider its pros and cons and the impact property ownership will have on your lifestyle both now and in the future.

● ●

YOUR PROPERTY PROS AND CONS

The complexity and uncertainty of the property market, not to mention the financial and lifestyle limitations home ownership may bring, can sometimes make us feel as if buying property isn't worth the headache. But securing your financial future, which includes knowing that you have a safe place of your own to call home, *can* be worth striving for.

In the space below, table your personal pros and cons towards property purchasing and ownership. How do they stack up against one another for you? Is this something that may change in the future?

Pros: what are some benefits you can see in buying and owning property?	Cons: what are some challenges you foresee in buying and owning property?

● ●

JESSICA, 29 – VIC

I already invest in shares and I don't want my first home to be an investment property. I want it to be an owner-occupier property for my partner and myself. My reason for wanting to buy a home, and not something to rent out, comes back to my values. Home is something that's important to me, so there's an emotional element. As someone who works in a creative space, both personally and for my freelance work, I want somewhere that I can feel comfortable in and that I can cultivate so it feels like home.

I have been relatively aggressive in saving for my deposit. Every dollar counts! I use She's on the Money crafty savings methods, such as selling items on Facebook Marketplace – it may just be $50 for an unwanted piece of furniture, or $30 for a piece of clothing, but if you keep it up, that money can soon add up big-time.

However, saving for me did come with a real sense of fatigue, so I stepped back from my hardcore savings plan a little bit, particularly in the last six months. I took international trips that I'd been wanting to go on and enjoy, and made the most of the first proper summer without Covid restrictions or constant rain.

I'd been saving so hard for so long, and it felt empowering at the time, because it was my choice that I made. But I realised I just wanted to breathe for a bit, so I did. That's partly why I haven't rushed into buying a house – I have been able to feel fully in control of the amount of money I was saving or investing.

● ● ● ● ● ●

TAKE NOTE

The real costs of buying property in Australia and the effects that broader economic conditions have on pricing and affordability can make things complicated.

....

Interest rates can and will fluctuate, as our long-term and recent history has shown, with the cash rate ranging from as high as 17.5 per cent in 1990 to as low as 0.1 per cent in 2022, followed by a series of 12 rate hikes over the subsequent year. Inflation and real wages' buying power also factor in.

....

It's important to be aware of the current set of economic conditions as well as remembering the long-term view. The longer you hold property, the smoother those bumps along the way may become.

....

Chapter 3

Your property goals

You spent Chapter 1 determining your why, and Chapter 2 stress-testing that decision as we looked at the painful reality of the current Australian property market. I think it's fair to say you've done your initial groundwork and really examined whether buying into the Great Australian Dream is for you. Now you should be in a great position to be both optimistic and realistic, to set specific goals with some timeframes and clear targets. So, let's look at how you might get into it.

KEY TERMS

home loan (or mortgage): most people can't afford to pay for a house entirely in cash they have stashed away, so they'll take out a loan for it, otherwise known as a mortgage.

deposit: to take out a loan, you'll need to bring some savings to the table. The standard expectation is that you'll bring 20 per cent of the total amount you'd like to borrow. So, for a $500,000 property that would mean a $100,000 deposit.

principal: this is the loan amount you borrow.

interest rate: this is what the lender charges you for borrowing money, calculated as a percentage of the debt they are carrying for you. The average home loan interest rate over the last 30 years in Australia has been around 7 per cent.

serviceability: your serviceability or capacity for 'servicing a loan' is a fancy way of looking at whether you can afford your monthly mortgage repayments.

Let's get clear on your goals

The first step to developing a property strategy is getting clear on your goals. Around here, we like our goals to be **SOTM** goals: **S**pecific, **O**ptimistic, **T**ime-based and **M**easurable. I have a whole chapter dedicated to this in my first book and my *She's on the Money Budget Journal* walks through how to set short-, medium- and long-term financial goals, so please refer to those resources if you'd like a deeper dive into SOTM goal setting. For now, let's focus on how that might look for you when it comes to property.

In the realm of property, SOTM goal setting has a lot to do with assessing where you're at in the buying cycle – first home, first investment, second property, etc. Are you single ready to mingle, or loved up with a bun in the oven? How's your career going – can you see yourself on the fast-track to making partner, have you just started a new business, or are you looking to take a backstep for a few years while you tend to personal matters? Are you ready to settle down in your forever home, or have you still got some big-world travelling to do? All of this will affect what you're looking for in a property and the timings around buying one. But no matter where you're at, it always pays to have a plan.

Creating a property plan

As a retired financial planner, I'm a fan of mapping things out – the name kinda gives it away – so of course I'm going to encourage you to make a plan in order to achieve your property goals. That said, as with any long-term goal, I like to follow US President Eisenhower's wisdom: 'In preparing for battle I have always found that plans are useless, but planning is indispensable.'

This is pure gold when it comes to long-term planning, especially around financial and estate planning and making not-so-little purchases (like buying a home), which are typically set to play out over a lifetime. You start out with a vision and a long-term goal, but there are often things that crop up along the way. You'll want to have thought these through, considered what impacts they might bring and have alternative tactics at the ready for when (not if) things change.

As with any strategy in life and finance, regular monitoring and review is *critical* – your life circumstances are liable to change at any moment, and most certainly over time. What works for you now won't hold true in five or ten years – you will be older and your earning capacity, relationship status and the world at large will have changed, hopefully improving, but equally possibly not.

That's why we can only devise best-laid plans that account for the best- and worst-case scenarios, and continually review and adjust accordingly. These are difficult topics to discuss with yourself and any partner – they may be some of the toughest conversations you'll have – but they'll also be the most rewarding, emotionally and practically, and help set you up on the right foundations. So don't be afraid to broach them – you've got this!

• •

DEVELOPING YOUR PROPERTY PLAN

Following the prompts below, I'd like you to start thinking through what you really need in a property versus what you might be dreaming of. Get started by jotting your initial thoughts down in the spaces provided. Then, as you progress through the buying-journey stages, come back to the prompts at various points and use them to continue developing your list. As a work-in-progress, this one may take many months, so refining is part of the process.

While we'll be going into many of these questions in much further detail in coming chapters, it's worth pulling out that lovely notebook you began earlier as you start pondering some of the following questions. Your answers to these prompts will likely change as you get deeper into the nitty-gritty, so keep these questions handy to review and revise as you start developing your property plan.

Hot tip: If you are looking at buying with a partner, have them complete this list for themselves separately, then compile your answers into a table and compare notes. Discuss which things are non-negotiables and where you might be happy to compromise to work out a plan that suits you both.

1. Usage

- Are you looking to buy to live in for yourself or to rent out and make money?
- Perhaps you want to run a business from home?
- Are you the type of person who loves to entertain and needs dedicated spaces to do so, or is home a place to rest your head?
- Do you need outdoor space – a balcony or a garden?
- Would you like to make money from renting a spare room, perhaps even Airbnb the whole place?

....

....

....

....

....

2. Who and how many?

- Are you wanting to buy with a partner/s or on your own?
- Is it important for you to retain complete control over the property (freestanding), or are you okay to be part of a building complex (as most apartments are)?
- For as long as you plan to have the property, can it accommodate the people and lifestyle you're looking for?
- Do you need a flexible floorplan than can morph from study, to nursery, to guestroom?
- How many people do you plan on having live there – now and in five years?
- How much storage might you need?
- Is parking necessary?
- Do you need to accommodate regular guests?
- How about pets?
- What impacts might these have on your business, flexibility, changes in circumstance and future plans for passing on inheritance?

....

....

....

....

....

3. Location
- How far are you willing to live from work?
- Is it accessible to the services you need i.e. health care, groceries, schools, cafes, bookstores, gym, parks?
- What's more important – your own private space at home, or instant access to a bustling nightlife?
- How often will you even be home to enjoy it?
- How much does external noise from local schools, roads, flight paths, or neighbours bother you?
- How close are you willing to be to your neighbours?
- What are the transport options for you and for visitors?

....

....

....

....

4. Demand
- Who else lives in the neighbourhood or is likely to in future?
- Does this property suit the general requirements of the local population, e.g. if a family suburb, does it have at least three bedrooms and some outdoor space (or could you make it)?
- How many new places are being built around you?
- How about support for the area's development – is it being improved or neglected?
- Is it the worst house, best street and an opportunity for growth, or are both the home and area in poor condition?

....

....

....

....

5. Aspect/Condition

No matter what property you buy, and especially on a lower budget, there'll always be something that requires immediate or long-term maintenance. Some things you can change, some you could change but at great expense, and others you're stuck with forever – like being a battle-axe block, or the direction it's facing. If the aspect makes it cold and dark, there's little you can do. And sun is lovely, but also harsh on paint. Some issues are cosmetic and some are structural. What could you live with, what couldn't you?

....

....

....

....

6. Purchasing costs

Saving for a deposit may be the most challenging part of getting into property. What compromises (if any) are you prepared to make financially/to your lifestyle to save for a deposit and what won't you budge on?

- What kind of budget are you working with?
- Do you have a deposit saved?
- How much do you earn and spend – this will dictate what kind of loan you can afford?
- What future financial impacts might you have to take into account, such as time off for family, travel, education?

Estimate your initial numbers:

....

....

....

....

7. Ongoing costs

If you are looking for a property that needs immediate renovations, have you factored this into your budget? You'll also need to factor in the ongoing costs of keeping and maintaining your property, over and above the living costs you will have already been paying as a renter. These can include: council rates, connecting and paying for utilities like water, insurance, strata levies (if applicable) and maintenance. And of course, your mortgage repayments.

- Are you looking to buy a standalone dwelling or an apartment; what kinds of costs would you need to factor in?
- Are you keen to buy a 'fixer-upper' or would you rather buy something that's done (either approach will impact your budget)?
- Looking at recent years, have you factored in interest rates changes and how they will impact your monthly loan repayments?

Estimate your ongoing costs – what can you afford both in mortgage repayments and ongoing holding and maintenance costs?

....

....

....

....

8. Timings

- When are you looking to buy – now, in the next 12 months, or in five years?
- Where are we at in the property cycle – broadly, and in the area you're looking at?

- What is the broader economy doing?
- How does this to impact your ability/desire to own property and service a loan?
- If you're planning to take time off work for any reason, have you factored this in?
- How about any unexpected changes in circumstance?

....

....

....

....

• •

And ... BREATHE

Those were all big, meaty questions that threw up lots to consider. You don't have to have all the answers right now; in fact, I expect you won't have many! So, if you need, jump up, pour yourself a nice warm tea and cuddle your cat/pillow/favourite human. Your whirling head is totally normal.

I know it's a lot, but seriously, don't stress! The SOTM community and I are here to support you, every step of the way. Also, The Property Playbook Facebook group can be a great resource to find a whole lotta pals just like you, asking all the same questions and sharing their worries and ideas.

Example: Blake, 27

Here's an example from our new imaginary friend, Blake. Let me introduce you ... Blake is 27 years old, earns $78,000 per annum and is looking to buy a place for themselves (no partner or dependants) near where they study and work as a researcher at Melbourne University.

Blake's draft property plan

1. Usage

- Buy to live in (not to rent out).
- Home sanctuary – light, comfort, warmth.
- Ideally, will include a dedicated study as I work from home.
- Would be nice (but not necessary) to have a small outdoor space.
- Entertaining/gathering space for eight and over (prefer hosting at home rather than going out).

2. Who and how many?

- Buy for myself, no partner currently.
- At least one extra bedroom for flexibility: flatmate, guests etc.
- Flat, apartment or townhouse (don't want/need whole house!).
- Accommodate me primarily, but possibly a flatmate and/or guests.
- Ideally two bed/study if possible.
- No parking needed.
- Good storage, including for my bike.

3. Location?

- Walking distance to public transport – commute to CBD.
- Less than ten minutes' walk to uni.
- Walking distance to a decent supermarket/grocer's market.
- Expect to have close neighbours, tight proximity.
- Close to parks for morning/weekend exercise.
- Some noise okay (expected) if location is convenient.

4. Demand?

- Central urban-ish location, limited supply, always popular.
- Additional boost being close to universities.
- Inner-city lifestyle, youngish singles/couples, fewer large families.
- Walking distance to uni, transport, shops, market, parks.

5. Condition/Aspect?
- Good structural condition (no funds for/interest in major reno).
- Old carpets and paint okay, happy to freshen up and make my own.
- North/north-east facing ideally, not south. Light-filled, decent outlook.
- Carpets in bedrooms/timber floor in living areas, or timber throughout.
- Can't be sterile modern, some inherent character needed.

6. Purchasing costs?
- $2,000 in shares, $10,000 in savings. (Long way to go!)
- Put money spent on holidays to this (no more overseas trips for a while).
- Look at changing current accommodation to save money – share house?
- Finish uni placement and in full-time employment by year end = more income.

7. Ongoing costs?
- Add extra upfront costs to my property spreadsheet to start factoring in (I had no idea!).
- Ensure affordable strata levy – no more than half my current rent.
- Ensure no expensive shared amenities for upkeep – avoid special levies.
- No need for garage/facilities, so make sure I'm not funding others' expense.

8. Timings?
- Save deposit over next 18 months (reduce expenses, increase income).
- Buy in two years.
- Intend to live in, but also a good investment because of unis.

Indoor research: window-shopping

Let's lighten things up a bit, yeah? It might not seem apparent so far, but there *are* some fun parts to this property game. One of the most enjoyable (at least, in my opinion) is getting up to speed with the market. Otherwise known as window-shopping!

A really great way to start breaking down your answers to many of the prompts above is to start looking around at property. And you don't even have to get off your couch to do it (at least not in the beginning). Grab your phone and open up Domain or Realestate.com.au (the two largest property-for-sale databases in Australia) and let your fingers do the walking.

Listings are advertisements

Before you start, let me let you in on a not-so-secret trade secret. Property listings are, fundamentally, ads. Essentially, agents are trying to make the property as appealing as possible, to get as many viewers through the door as they can. Images are frequently shot with wide-angle lenses to make the space look bigger, and photos are always cropped and Photoshopped. Likewise with the property's price guide, which, especially at the beginning of a campaign, is set to entice people along to test the market.

Real estate terms decoded

Real estate jargon	Actually means
Convenient	So close to the train station you'll get a free massage every time one rolls by.
Cosy/intimate	So small you can't swing a cat.
Cute/adorable	Kitsch decoration and tiny to boot.
Harbour views	Glimpses of blue that could be mistaken for sky; maybe is sky?

Has character	It's really ugly.
An 'opportunity not to be missed'	You're probably going to have to knock it down.
Waterfront	Street occasionally floods.
Investment opportunity	You probably won't want to live here.

Only after assessing the buyers' views on the place can the agent start refining to a realistic guide. My friend, they're not trying to be tricky here (not usually, anyway). The truth is that the market will pay what the market will pay, and it's only after engaging with potential buyers that the agent can get a good idea of the price point. But that doesn't really help you when you're trying to get a realistic feel for what your budget can afford. The only way that you can start educating yourself to get closer to the mark is to have a look at what similar properties recently sold for.

Use filters

So how do you make it work in your favour? Filters are your best friend here. Of course, we use them to narrow our search field to match our house-hunting criteria – for location (suburb), price, bedrooms, parking, dwelling type (house, apartment) etc. You can also use keywords to add anything unusually specific you're looking for, such as focusing in on a particular street.

The key here is to narrow, but then expand. For example, when I'm in my initial research phase, I tick the 'include surrounding suburbs' box for location and select a range for the number of bedrooms both above and below my ideal. Agents classify their listings in all sorts of strange ways – one lists a place as having 2 beds, another as having 1 bed and study; one counts an awkward off-street strip next to the bins as 'parking', while another only counts enclosed garaging. That's why, later, you'll want to inspect your shortlist in person. For now, we're just building our list.

Hot tip: Most people only search on 'For Sale' properties as this is the default view, but 'Sold' listings are waaay more useful – at this stage anyway. Instead of searching 'For Sale', use the 'Sold' filter to retrieve a list of all the sales in the area. This will help you build a realistic view on pricing. One thing to watch out for is the sold date. While it's helpful to compare the prices over time, you'll usually find that your buying power today will be quite different to that of five years (or even five months!) ago.

● ●

START GATHERING DATA

At this point, it could be helpful to start a spreadsheet, though you could also the 'star' in the app to make your shortlist if that's more your style. I like a spreadsheet as it gives me an immediate visual of all the properties and comparison points, along with space to add my own notes. If you're a spreadsheet fan like me, you can also 'sort by' criteria later when wanting to narrow your focus.

Let's use this example, created by our new friend Blake.

Suburb	Type	Beds	Baths	Parking	Aspect	Size	Price
Carlton	Flat	2	1	1	E	65 sqm	$550,000
	Notes: Large open-plan, park views						
Carlton	Apartment	2	2	1	W	79 sqm	$625,000
	Notes: Modern building, balcony						
Carlton	Apartment	2	2	0	S	45 sqm	$435,000
	Notes: Tiny, balcony, great location						
Carlton	Apartment	2	2	1	N	48 sqm	$425,000
	Notes: Light, balcony, basic, small						
Carlton	Apartment	2	1	1	NW	58 sqm	$415,000
	Notes: Roomy, feels very urban						

Carlton	Apartment	2	2	1	S	75 sqm	$615,000
	Notes: Brand-new, balcony, roomy						
Carlton	Apartment	2	1	0	NE	52 sqm	$310,000
	Notes: Two-storey, small living room						
						Average Price	**$482,143**

Source: sample 'sold' listings on Domain, Jan–May 2023

• •

Outdoor research: your new Saturday morning

The next step after online window shopping is, of course, inspecting. Nothing beats the power of your senses, and it's only when you're physically onsite that you can smell, see, touch and feel a place, to really get its true measure.

For many, a property purchase will be the most they spend on any single item in their lifetime, so it should not be an impulse late-night buy. Not that you can readily buy property with one click of a button (yet!), but I *have* known people to purchase property sight unseen from the other side of the world – something I personally wouldn't recommend unless you have a support network on the ground who are tried-and-true *and* professionally qualified *and* have no personal interest (commission, I'm looking at you) in the purchase. The stakes are just too high.

So, just for fun – nothing too serious at this stage – try and pop into a few inspections in the area you're interested in over the next month or two. Later, when you click into the more intentional phase of your buying journey, inspections will become a whole lot more serious. We'll go into detail in Chapter 8 on how to take a more critical approach and get more specific about what to look for during an inspection.

But for now, pick a few listed properties that meet your budget and preferences and check them out in leisurely style, with your Saturday morning coffee in hand. This will help you get a real feel for exactly what 'south-facing' feels like at 11 am in mid-winter, and just how tight a 2m x 1.8m room actually is. From there, you can fine-tune your 'must-haves' and 'non-negotiables' further.

Hot tip: Even if you are just dream-shopping during your lunchbreak, keep updating your spreadsheet regularly. You may not want to buy immediately, but getting into the practice of this research will set you up with the knowledge that Future You needs, in order to make an educated decision.

A first look at your finances

Now that you've pulled together the beginnings of a shortlist of potential dream homes, it's time to start thinking about your budget – or, more realistically, your deposit. Your 'Sold' shortlist will have given you price guides for the types of properties you're interested in. Question is: can you afford them?

There are many upfront costs to buying property in addition to the house price. As previously mentioned, this is not the kind of money that anyone will just having lying around, so you'll need to approach someone to loan you the money by way of a home loan (mortgage). Before a lender will look at you, you'll need to prove to them that you're a safe bet. This is where a deposit comes in.

To get a home loan, you'll need to have saved around 20 per cent of the purchase price to use as a deposit. This shows the lender that you have the budgeting skills to have saved a decent chunk of money and will likely be able to service (pay off) a loan. Your deposit percentage can vary (in some cases, to as low at 5 per cent), but there are many things the banks – and you – should take into consideration when deciding upon your initial contribution, as well as various loans and schemes you could access to bring this down. We'll get into those details in Chapter 4. For now, 20 per cent is a sensible starting point which brings its own advantages – and whatever you don't use upfront can go into your post-purchase Emergency Fund.

● ●

YOUR DEPOSIT GOAL

To get yourself a savings guide, you could go ahead and calculate the rate against every property in your shortlist and come up with a range. Alternatively, you could determine the average price of all the properties and what 20 per cent of that would be, to work towards a single guidepost.

Create a spreadsheet of your own, plugging in the prices of the properties you're looking at, to work out your 20 per cent deposit, and there you have it: a savings goal – perhaps the biggest one you'll set in your life! It may seem a bit overwhelming right now, but so many in our She's on the Money community have achieved it – millennial singles, DINKs and families – so I have every belief that it's possible for YOU too.

Example – Blake's 20 per cent deposit

Price	Notes	Deposit
$550,000	Large open-plan, park views	$110,000
$625,000	Modern building, balcony	$125,000
$435,000	Tiny, balcony, great location	$87,000
$425,000	Light, balcony, basic, small	$85,000
$415,000	Roomy, feels very urban	$83,000
$615,000	Brand-new, balcony, roomy	$123,000
$310,000	Two-storey, small living room	$62,000
	Average Deposit	$96,429

● ●

At this early stage, you might feel a little disheartened by what you can realistically afford. Keep in mind that if this is your first home, it will unlikely be your ultimate dream home. Baby steps, my friend! It's great to have long-term goals for the future, so by all means, crank that vision board and imagine the house of your dreams, but also get to work taking positive action. By starting small, it's quite possible to upgrade your properties over time. Just remember that always, *always*, your dream home is the one you can afford.

Your repayments

Let's look at what you'll need to borrow. It's just the price of the house, right? Wrong.

There are several additional costs you must factor into your property purchase which will be added to your mortgage. As well as the agreed purchase price of the property, you will have to pay government transfer/stamp duty, legal fees, establishment and registration fees and, if your deposit is less than 20 per cent, compulsory lender's mortgage insurance (LMI), unless you're covered by a government scheme. (I'll cover these off in detail in Chapter 6, so let's not get too caught up on them here.)

For now, let's simply look at the cost breakdown in order to get a decent gauge for what your monthly repayment could look like. We'll also assume you are going to take out a standard owner-occupier mortgage that pays back both the principal and interest over a 30-year term (again, this will be covered in Chapter 6).

First, let's add in the extra costs that will be added to your mortgage. Following, is a guide based on a $500,000 purchase in Queensland, as provided by Realestate.com.au.[26] It assumes a lot of things, but the reality is that these costs are guides only, based on averages for such services and fees. Each state/territory, and lender, sets their own fees and rates, so you'll need to check with the relevant authorities for where the property is being purchased. When it comes time, make sure you get exact prices from your providers.

As a rough guide, here's a quick glance at various monthly mortgage repayments based on different percentage interest rates with a 10 per cent deposit (for an owner-occupier paying principal and interest on a 30-year term).

Additional costs to purchase a $500,000 property

First home buyer

Purchase price	$500,000	Loan repayments on $516,807	
Stamp duty (first home buyer)	$0		
Building/pest inspection	$600	3.5 %	$2,321
Mortgage registration fee	$187	5%	$2,775
Transfer fee	$1,120	7.5%	$3,614
Loan application fee	$600	10%	$4,536
LMI (waived with some grants)	$12,000		
Council and water rates	$500		
Conveyancing and legal fees	$1,800		
SUB TOTAL hidden costs	**$16,807**		
TOTAL COST to purchase house	**$516,807**		

Non-first home buyer

Purchase price	$500,000	Loan repayments on $525,557	
Stamp duty (non-first home buyer)	$8,750		
Building/pest inspection	$600	3.5 %	$2,360
Mortgage registration fee	$187	5%	$2,822
Transfer fee	$1,120	7.5%	$3,675
Loan application fee	$600	10%	$4,613
LMI (with only 10% deposit)	$12,000		
Council and water rates	$500		
Conveyancing and legal fees	$1,800		
SUB TOTAL hidden costs	$25,557		
TOTAL COST to purchase house	$525,557		

As you can see, taking on a mortgage is a big commitment, and as our parents love to keep reminding us, 'back in the day', mortgage interest rates hit an all-time high of 15.5 per cent. Very few experts believe that will happen again, but we can't avoid the reality that our interest rates began creeping up post-Covid, so we'd be foolish not expect them to stay ouchie for a while – and if there's one thing SOTM pals ain't, it's foolish. When we do our sums it's sensible to factor in a conservative average interest rate across the life of our loans.

As a reminder, the average mortgage interest rate in Australia, historically, sits around 7 per cent over the long term (typically a few points higher, and sometimes lower, than the official cash rate). It averaged 6.87 per cent from 1990 until 2023, reaching an all-time high of 15.5 per cent in September of 1990 and a record low of 2.14 per cent in March of 2021.[27]

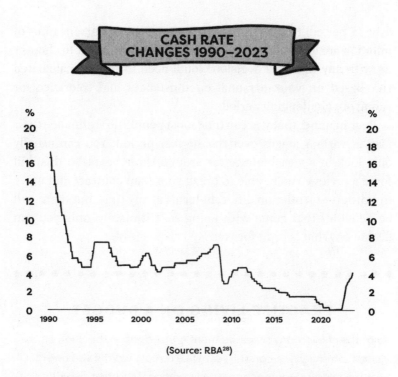

CASH RATE CHANGES 1990–2023

(Source: RBA[28])

'So, Victoria, what's a sensible interest rate to budget for?'

Depending on how risk-averse you are, you could calculate your budgets based on paying back an historic average rate of interest (e.g. 7 per cent) over the life of your loan. If you prefer to determine how you could keep servicing a loan (meeting your repayments) if it were to reach an unusually high point, you may like to factor in your repayments based on a buffer of 10 per cent. If you were very defensive, you could factor in your serviceability at the all-time highest mortgage rate of 15.5 per cent.

The latter is a safer strategy, sure, but the problem with it is that very few (if any) other buyers will be doing that, so you'll end up bidding against people who, having based their affordability on lower rates, are putting more spending money on the table. Also, most experts agree that the chances of Australians paying over 15 per cent interest on their home loans at current rates of inflation are low. But you can never say never! So, what to choose? As with any financial decision, you'll need to make a calculated risk based on your personal circumstances and tolerance for riding out challenging periods.

Bear in mind, that you can (and most people do) refinance their loan at various stages over the 30-year period. You can usually only lock in a variable rate for around three years, so this will force a review. You're able to break your loan contract and move to a different lender on different terms at any time, but there will be penalties that come with doing so. Ultimately, only you can decide on what is right for you.

• •

PRACTISE LIVING ON A BUDGET

No matter how many times we mention 'budget' in the She's on the Money community, it can still seem like a scary word if you aren't taking a mindful approach to your spending. The good news is, you haven't bought a house yet. (See, I told you we'd find all the upsides!) But in all seriousness, if you're just now embarking on your first home-buying journey, you have the benefit of time on your side.

As the above calculations showed, affording a home doesn't end with your deposit. So before you land yourself in a big hot mess, why not take the homeowner's lifestyle for a cheeky practice run? Before you're locked into the pressure of a mortgage for real, jump online to any bank's mortgage repayment calculator to get a picture of what a mortgage repayment for your home could look like – remembering to include the extra costs outlined above – and practise putting away that amount of money each month.

If funds are tight, and they probably will be if you're also paying rent, then to be fair on yourself you could subtract some of your current rent money from this amount. That said, owning property is not just about paying off the mortgage. There are other regular costs you must allocate funds to, things like council and water rates, strata levies (if relevant) and ongoing maintenance. Unlike investing in shares, property has ongoing expenses which, if you're renting, your landlord is currently paying for you. So, if you want to be super-savvy, keep paying your rent and consider this the amount you'd allocate to these ongoing expenses once you buy property. Then see if you can save the mortgage amount on top of this.

Give yourself at least six months to a year on this program while asking yourself these questions:

- Can I live comfortably on the remaining amount?
- Am I sacrificing anything significant to afford this?
- Am I significantly less happy living this way?
- How long do I reasonably think I can continue living like this?

• •

Reviewing your priorities

Whether you're going sassy solo-sister style or buying in partnership, it's crucial to work through your list and prioritise what's important to you. One thing worth learning early is that there will be compromises. Unless a mysterious rich aunt gifts you an inheritance out of the blue, or you win the lottery, I can almost guarantee that you won't be able to have everything on your wishlist. Having just had a quick look at the cost to get into property, I'm sure you can see why.

So, upfront, it's worth figuring out what your non-negotiables are and where you might be happy to make some adjustments. Remember that the more properties you see, the more you will refine your list. So, stay open and continue to review as you go along.

If you're buying with a partner, friend or family member, it's important to loop them into the process. Ideally, they will have created their own separate notebook and/or spreadsheets and are personally working through the prompts in this chapter to figure out their own values, goals and lifestyle needs when it comes to property. Once you've independently made your own wishlists and property shortlists, it's time to sit down and compare notes.

No doubt there'll be some areas in which your beliefs, values and goals differ. That's okay. It's perfectly healthy. The best time to talk through these differences is now, when the whole exercise is still hypothetical. Same goes for the more serious stuff, like how to set up your ownership structure, planning for inheritance and having the right insurances in place (we'll get to those in Chapter 7).

For now, it's important to begin the conversation and learn how to negotiate your priorities so that everyone's looked after, happy and satisfied. If that conversation is only with yourself, self-reflection and regular check-ins are just as important. Ensuring you are still healthy, happy and onboard with perhaps the biggest commitment of your life is, well you know, kinda important.

● ●

REVIEW AND PRIORITISE

Look back over your initial list and review and refine, based on what you have discovered through your inspections and research. To help prioritise their importance, add a note according to what's below.

Non-negotiable. These are the things which the property must have for you to consider it. Try to keep this list small so you can keep your options open! For example: number of bedrooms, distance from a train station, off-street parking.

A dealbreaker. The things you explicitly don't want in a property. For example: close to a main road, in a rural area, no office space.

Bonuses. Potential characteristics which aren't make-or-break for you. They could be nice, but if not available, it won't be the end of the world. For example: hardwood floors, ensuite bathroom, open-plan kitchen and dining.

Hot tip: If you're buying with someone, have them mark their own priorities separately, then compare. See where you might each need to compromise to reach a final agreed list.

Let's use and develop Blake's list from earlier as an example. Note how their list has developed since their original ideas. Yours will likely change too as you inspect properties and refine your needs. You also might need to break out certain attributes onto their own line in order to prioritise them as you prefer.

Example: Blake's final list

Feature	Must-have	Dealbreaker	Bonus
Work-from-home	✓		
Entertaining			✓
Internal laundry	✓		
Functional kitchen	✓		
Small outdoor space			✓
Airconditioning			✓
Two bedrooms	✓		
Study			✓
Bike storage	✓		
15-min walk to uni	✓		
North-facing, light and bright			✓

Feature	Must-have	Dealbreaker	Bonus
South-facing, cold and dark		✓	
Major renovation needed		✓	
$500K purchase, $800/qtr levies		✓	
Buy in two years			✓

Your list

Non-negotiables	Dealbreakers	Bonus features

Alternatively, you could write it out like this.

My non-negotiables
- Work-from-home, cosy home, sunny
- 2 bedroom minimum
- Space to store bike (internal/secure external)
- Internal laundry and functional kitchen
- No more than 15-minute walk to uni

My dealbreakers
- Priced more than $500,000 – no deal
- Strata fees higher than $800/qtr – fancy facilities not needed
- No major renovation or significant upkeep – requires minimal maintenance
- South-facing, cold/dark

My bonuses
- Extra small study/sunroom/nook
- Heritage features/character/north-facing
- Timings: 2 years
- Small outdoor space: courtyard/balcony
- Aircon (heating/cooling)

• •

Satisfying your needs

With property, possibly for more than any other purchase, it's important to consider your *needs* above your *wants* as these will be critical in helping you find a place within your budget. As I say, the right house for you is the house you can afford, both today and tomorrow when – perhaps interest rates, or your income or your lifestyle – may look very different.

• • • • • •

LIZ, 36 – NSW

During my 20s, I wasn't interested in owning property and always felt like it was out of reach for me, as a single female. My parents raised me with the belief I needed a dual income to buy – that a mortgage is 'bad debt' which needs two people to service. I never felt empowered to do it alone, so I spent my money on fun things and good times instead.

Fast-forward to my 30s and I'm now a solo parent with a nesting instinct and desire to lay roots after the birth of my daughter. To start saving, I rented a studio apartment close to my parents, started contributing to my super with the First Home Super Saver scheme and sought the help of a financial adviser.

We ran a few scenarios, but ultimately I decided to rentvest. Enlisting the help of an ethical B-corp mortgage-broking team and an awesome female team of buyer's agents in Hobart, we found a beautiful property within a few days and I put in an offer. Having them to hold my hand throughout the offer process, building inspection, valuation and settlement really empowered me and my decision-making.

Now, I'm the proud owner of a house with a beautiful veggie garden in Hobart that perhaps one day my daughter and I can enjoy!

JELENA, 32 – QLD

I came to Australia as a refugee in 1997. To date, nobody in my family owns a home, nor has great financial literacy, and I was never taught how to save, invest, or about entering the property market. In my late 20s, in the aftermath of a breakup, I decided to educate myself about money and finances. I set a goal three years ago to buy a home.

In December 2022, I purchased my first home in Brisbane using the NHFIC (National Housing Finance and Investment Corporation) scheme. I spoke with my partner's father to understand the process, lessen my anxiety and get some guidance I could trust. He helped me understand my serviceability and an estimate for repayment amounts, then assisted in negotiations and paperwork when it came time to buy.

In the last six months, I have done a mini renovation, this time with my father's help. From five types of linoleum on the floors in different shades of brown and orange, to now fresh white stone tiles throughout, the place looks bright and almost like a new home on the inside!

I feel very privileged having been given the opportunities I have been afforded, and like I am a catalyst – building on my family's resilience and sacrifices to create financial literacy and, hopefully, wealth for future generations.

● ● ● ● ● ●

TAKE NOTE

Plans are useless, but planning is indispensable – so take the time to put together a solid property plan that can be flexible over time.

....

Thinking through and getting your property priorities down on paper will help you shape up a realistic property goal. There *will* be compromises. Remember: your dream property is the one you can afford!

....

Time and market conditions may mean you can upgrade your first property some years down the line. No guarantees, of course . . . but start small, keep working away, and who knows where you might end up.

....

Chapter 4

Real-world strategies for buying property

Now that you have a realistic goal, you're in a great position to start taking active steps towards achieving it. It will require some strategic moves and a bit of hard yakka, but you've got this!

This is where we tune into SOTM-savvy tactics and get to work. While the boomers may have got in early and stockpiled their wealth into quarter-acre blocks, we millennials have fresh, new ways of thinking and approaching property that they wouldn't dare try. I'll go through these in this chapter and also outline some tried-and-true methods to give you a bunch of tools, tips and tricks to build out an approach that works for you.

There *are* ways and means for all us millennials, no matter whether single or loved-up, to get our feet in the door. We just have to be smart and open-minded in our approach.

KEY TERMS

co-ownership: purchasing a property together with friend/s or family.

exchanging contracts: this the moment a house sale becomes legal. The buyer and seller exchange signed contracts (which typically also requires that the buyer pays a deposit, e.g. 10 per cent). From that moment, the sale becomes binding – conditional upon all the terms specified in the contract.

first home buyer schemes: there are several state-based and federal government assistance schemes to help first home buyers get their first home.

LMI – lender's mortgage insurance: deposits less than 20 per cent of the purchase price are generally charged LMI to cover the risk of defaulting. This can be reduced with some first home buyer schemes.

rentvesting: purchasing an affordable investment property elsewhere, while continuing to rent in the city to maintain one's current job and lifestyle.

tiny home: smaller-than-normal dwellings (sometimes mobile) – usually a single room combining living, dining, sleeping, along with a separate bathroom.

vendor: the person selling the property.

Affordability

At the end of the day, what you can buy comes down to what you can afford – both by way of deposit and ongoing home loan repayments, as well as the costs of ongoing fees, maintenance and upkeep. For many on single incomes, even the lowest-priced housing close to our work and lifestyle seem completely out of reach. So, what do we do then?

First home buyer government schemes

Aware of the difficulties Australians face in getting into the property market, the Australian Government has various schemes in place to assist first home buyers. The details of these change over time, so it's worth getting in touch with a specialist – mortgage brokers are great – to ensure you're up to speed with the latest when it comes time for you to buy.

At the time of writing, both the federal and state/territory governments have a range of first home buyer assistance grants and financial support schemes in place. Since these are regularly updated and come with a slew of eligibility requirements, we'll touch on them briefly here, just to give you an idea of what assistance you may be able to access, but it's important to jump online and/or speak to an expert to nut out the finer details as they pertain to you at the time you're ready to buy. A good starting point is the government website: firsthome.gov.au.

State and territory first home buyer grants and schemes

Each Australian state and territory has its own first home buyer assistance packages, with some states offering multiple pathways. You'll need to review each in detail depending on your needs and where you live. Since these schemes typically require its recipient to live in the home that they've bought, the scheme applies to the state/territory in which the property is located.

The eligibility criteria vary state by state; however, similar guidelines apply. Depending on which grant or scheme you opt into, a first home buyer eligible home may be a new or established house, home unit, flat or other type of self-contained fixed dwelling, and in some locations, land. Some are grants, some are schemes that waive or reduce stamp duty and/or LMI.

Most applications for these schemes must be made through your lender, not directly with the government, with limited places released at the start of each new financial year. Once you have taken up an offer, you must generally close the deal within a set timeframe or forfeit your place – usually within three months or so. As such, it pays to begin these conversations early to ensure you can take advantage of the schemes and that the timings work in your favour.

Typically, the following requirements apply:

- You must never have owned property in Australia before.
- This must be the first time you've applied for the scheme.
- You must be an Australian citizen or permanent resident.
- You must be an individual (not a company or trust).
- Pricing limits apply – anywhere between $650,000 and $1 million.
- You must move in within six to twelve months of buying and live there for at least six months.

Under many schemes the following types of properties are ineligible:

- Primary production land.
- Land used for business or a business premises.
- Holiday homes.

Federal schemes

At the federal level, there are several policies and grants aimed at helping first home buyers with specific eligibility criteria for each policy. Once again, these are subject to change, so while I'll outline some current options below, please review the schemes and speak to an expert when the time comes for you to secure a mortgage.

First Home Buyer Guarantee (FHBG). This allows eligible first home buyers to get a home loan with just a 5 per cent deposit and avoid the extra cost of LMI while accessing an interest rate as if you were paying a 20 per cent deposit.

Regional First Home Buyer Guarantee (RFHBG). This aims to support eligible first home buyers to purchase a home in a regional area. Approved property types include existing houses, townhouses or apartments, house and land packages, land with a separate contract to build a home, and off-the-plan apartments or townhouses. The scheme enables an eligible home buyer to purchase a home with as little as 5 per cent deposit without paying LMI.

Family Home Guarantee (FHG). This aims to support eligible single parents with at least one dependent child to buy a home, whether that single parent is a first home buyer or a previous homeowner. The FHG enables an eligible home buyer to purchase a home with as little as 2 per cent deposit without paying LMI.

First Home Super Saver Scheme (FHSS). Another helpful option for some first home buyers, this policy allows eligible buyers to make extra contributions to their super funds ($15,000 a year, up to a maximum of $50,000) and later withdraw them to use towards a house deposit. The benefit of accruing savings within super is that they are taxed at 15 per cent instead of at your usual tax rate.

Other government support

What if you're not a first home buyer? Some states and territories offer additional help for *anyone* looking to buy property. It pays to conduct your own research, both online and by speaking to property professionals. Refer to the Appendix for links to helpful websites.

Thinking outside the box

In addition to government schemes, here at She's on the Money, we love to think outside the box. Here are some SOTM-savvy millennial strategies that offer fresh thinking and new opportunities to buy property in today's world.

Tiny homes

Recent years have seen a surge of people gravitating towards tiny homes as a new home ownership strategy. Tiny homes not only offer a more affordable entry point into the property market, but also pay back big-time in environmental benefits, both of which are important for SOTM-savvy buyers.

Tiny homes, as the name suggests, are small and compact houses ranging from about 10 to 50 sqm, designed to maximise space and energy efficiency. Sometimes they're built on wheels or trailers for portability (unlike, say, a granny flat). One of their most obvious benefits is that they're significantly cheaper to both buy and run than traditional homes.

Tiny homes can be bought or built for a fraction of the cost of a regular house. While they vary in price, they start from around $75,000 – about the same as many home-loan deposits. Size-wise and by design, tiny homes are also highly energy-efficient, typically featuring insulation, solar panels and other eco-friendly features, a win for both the environment and your back pocket.

For those into the minimalist trend, tiny homes are bang on target. Their designs maximise functionality, thereby limiting the need for excessive gadgets or furniture. The floorplan puts a ban on clutter and excessive consumption and encourages its inhabitants to live on what's at hand – often the bare necessities. Still, though many tiny homes are regionally located, living tiny doesn't mean you have to live like a nomad, far from civilisation, foraging berries and bathing in rivers. A lot of people set up tiny homes in cities, say, on the back of a family member's property or as an additional building on an existing property.

For some, this is a long-term lifestyle enabling multi-generational families to remain close while saving costs. For others, it's a short-term plan aimed at saving a deposit they can put down on a larger place. For those who already own property, adding a freestanding private dwelling to their block may be an excellent source of rental income. Some landowners simply lease a corner of their block to tiny-home owners; rent for a fixed address and utilities.

This new-world approach to housing benefits people in many ways. It can work out cheaper than renting an entire apartment or home, particularly if you have the means to buy your tiny home outright, thereby reducing ongoing accommodation expenses. If yours is a mobile tiny home, you can move around as you please for work or travel purposes – a kind of luxury caravan – perhaps the perfect option for those of you whose value exercises showed a high need for flexibility and spontaneity, coupled with housing security.

TINY HOMES

Cons of tiny homes

Of course, there are some downsides and risks to living tiny, such as the fact that tiny homes are . . . well, tiny. If you're used to living in larger spaces or have bags of possessions, it might be difficult to scale your lifestyle back to accommodate the tiny space. There are also certain building regulations and requirements that must be met, depending on where you want to set up your tiny home. Some areas may require a permit or compliance with building codes to build or to park. Also, take note that insurers and the government treat mobile and impermanent homes differently from fixed dwellings – a sad fact many discovered after the 2022 Lismore floods.

In terms of wealth creation, although having a tiny home means you will own your own living space without a mortgage, tiny living is still a fairly niche market, so if you decide to sell your home down the track, you might struggle to find a buyer and may not get more than what you paid for it. Also, it's currently not possible to get a home loan for a tiny house – you'll need alternative financing; either drawing on the equity in an existing home loan on the same block, or a construction loan – where the funds are made available in stages as progress payments to the builder.[29] As always, it's best to discuss your options with a lender or mortgage broker.

If your tiny home is mobile, it's also important to know how to hook up it up to utilities like water and electricity, and how to deal with the sewerage system (yep, no traditional toilets here). This can be difficult depending on your set-up location. And if you're someone who places high value on security, a tiny home might not satisfy that if you are still in the renting game in terms of the land you park it on.

Your very own share house

After uni, you may be so sick of living with people you barely know while tidying up their mess that you never want to think about it again. Then again, maybe it was the best time of your life and you keep wondering how you might be able to do it forever. Regardless of your uni-life experiences, don't let them turn you off the thought of co-ownership. Grown-up house-sharing can be with family, a friend or a whole tribe. More people than ever are making this a reality.[30]

As we learned in Chapter 2, with most couples nowadays throwing their double salary behind their house-buying offers, single-salaried bidders are being left behind. And if you're not part of a couple, nor perhaps ever plan to be, where does that leave you?

One way to fight against this is to co-own property with friends or family. Increasingly, more people are buying as 'tenants in common', which gives them joint (collective) and several (individual) ownership rights over a property. We'll take a deep dive into those terms in Chapter 7 when we review property ownership structures, but for now, let's focus on why you might consider buying a property with someone else.

Home ownership immediately becomes a lot more affordable, which means you can get into the market sooner. Having someone to go through the process of buying with can be a great mental and emotional support too. You've also got your co-owner when it comes to all the costs in maintaining and renovating a property, and someone to divide chores with.

CO-OWNERSHIP

Cons of a share house

Not everything is sunshine and rainbow daquiris, though. Buying a share house means you have to take into account your property partners' must-haves and can't-stands when choosing what to purchase, and these may not align exactly with your own. You'll have to negotiate on how to manage the place too, and what to spend on fixes and renovations can be challenging if you're working from different budgets and value systems. You are also stuck in a long-term partnership with someone who's not your life partner, and who may, now or in the future, have a different lifestyle to you.

● ●

PONDERING CO-OWNERSHIP

If co-ownership is something you're thinking about, consider these questions:

1. Who might you consider buying property with?
2. Who would you never buy property with?
3. What kind of lifestyle are you imagining? Ask your potential co-owner to write theirs down separately. Are your lifestyles a good match? What if one of you changes down the track?
4. How will you manage the chores? The bills? What if one of you gets ill and can't contribute?
5. How might you prevent arguments over decisions on maintenance and renovations?
6. How would you come to an agreement if one of you wants to sell, but the other doesn't?

● ●

Rentvesting

What if I told you there could be a way to afford property, even while house prices appear to hike forever upwards? A chance to get your foot in the door without having to move away from work, your friends and everything you love about where you live, other than its astronomical house prices? Hello, rentvesting!

Rentvesting is a strategy that's about creating future wealth, and less about what you personally want in a property. Using this approach, you a) rent a property to live in that suits your lifestyle, and b) purchase an investment property that's right for your budget. Your aim is to purchase a property that you can afford, that will pay its way and that will increase in value over time.

Our rentvesting goal should sound like: *'I want my property to have the strongest capital growth and rental income so I can sell it in the future to fund a home that is closer to my dream home.'*

This takes the emotion out of the decision. When rentvesting, we really don't care if the property has our dream kitchen or room for a dog. What we do care about is purchasing a property that's attractive to tenants (to cover our holding costs) and has strong appeal come sale time. The idea is that we should end up with more money in our back pocket than we started out.

For example, it could be somewhere that is low maintenance and close to public transport. Ideally, there may be plans for future improvements by the council, such as regreening an old tip, that in time will beautify the area and add value. Ideally, you would also make low-cost improvements to increase your property's appeal and value. All these things contribute to capital growth.

Rentvesting may not be a strategy our parents had to consider, but don't let that trick you into thinking it is a less legitimate way to buy a property. If you do decide you want to invest in property and rentvesting is an option that gets you there, then once you've weighed up all the pros and cons and determined that this could work, I'm glad we've found you a way in!

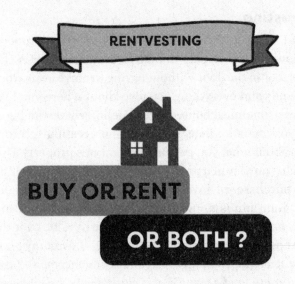

Cons of rentvesting

Rentvesting is a long-term strategy. It isn't perfect, but neither is any investment, property or otherwise. When you rentvest, you must be strategic about your property choice to get the best return on your investment possible – there are no guarantees. Plus, you'll still be in your own rental home, subject to all of the challenges that come with tenancy.

In addition, keep in mind when doing your sums that $1,000 earned in rental income is not strictly equivalent to $1,000 paid in rent, for example. Rental income is taxable (the rate will depend on your specific situation) whereas rent that is paid for a home comes out of post-tax income.

Finally, when you sell the property and it earns a profit, it will be subject to a capital gains tax because it isn't your primary residence.

Nevertheless, as you can see, if you're willing to do your research and consider other routes into the market, there are more options out there than you may have initially thought.

The property-purchasing process

Of course, the most important part of your property strategy is nailing the purchase. No matter what type of property you choose to buy, who you choose to buy it with, where you buy it, or even the specific way in which you buy it, there are certain stages that every buyer will go through.

If this all feels a little overwhelming, don't panic. This is just a short overview of the steps in the process – a primer, if you will. In the next chapter I'll introduce you to your dream team – the people who can help you through each of these steps. But first let's look briefly at what's involved.

1. Ready to buy – what do I do first?
Once you've decided to buy property, you'll want to engage the two most important consultants on your team: your solicitor/conveyancer and your lender/mortgage broker. In their respective lanes, each can guide you through the stresses involved in buying real estate. It's best to know what you can and can't do when dealing with a real estate agent and you should be aware of your cooling-off rights before you enter into a contract to purchase property.

2. The contract for sale of land
As a buyer, you can expect a real estate agent to provide you with a contract of sale. It will contain all the details of the property, including: a zoning certificate showing whether it's been zoned as residential or for some other purpose; a full title search showing any easements or restrictions that affect the use of the property, including any mortgages or other matters affecting the title; and a sewer diagram to show if or where the sewer main crosses the property.

The contract also contains a description of all inclusions to be sold with the property and the date of settlement (or completion) to take place. Everything can be negotiated; for example, that settlement should be 12 weeks post exchange, or if a vendor wants to take a beloved light fitting. (Unless otherwise noted, all fixtures and fittings should be included, so unless it's noted in the contract, that light fitting is all yours.)

That said, not all things that affect the sale will be written into the contract. Several matters enshrined in legislation are not spelled out in the written contract, so unless you're fully across these, it's best to have a solicitor/conveyancer explain the full effect before you sign.

3. Building and pest inspections

Before you commit yourself to a purchase, you need to decide whether you want to get any inspections done, as the contract does not cover the condition of its buildings. If you're buying a house, you will want to know that the building is structurally sound and that it's not infected by termites or other structural pests. An experienced inspector is invaluable in advising on structural problems that may not be readily visible – both building and pest. It may be worth enquiring whether their professional indemnity insurance will allow you to make a claim in case they miss something critical.

4. Strata inspections

When buying a unit, townhouse or villa, you are buying into a strata scheme (more on this in Chapter 7). You may want to know, for example, if there are any plans for building works, and will that require a special levy? To get a clearer picture of the whole complex, you should obtain an inspection of the books and records of the owners' corporation, commonly called a strata inspection. There are professional firms who specialise in this.

5. Finance

Before you apply for a loan, you should do a budget to help you work out how much you can afford to pay each week on loan repayments. There are many places you can apply for a loan: banks, credit unions, mortgage lenders or a finance broker. It's essential to shop around – don't just apply to the bank you've had an account at since you were seven – and do your homework on the many different kinds of loans available (which we'll explore more in Chapter 6) before you apply.

6. Exchanging contracts

When the seller and buyer have agreed on a price and the conditions of the sale, the contracts are drawn up in duplicate – one copy is signed by the seller and another by the buyer. When they're exchanged (either through solicitors or the real estate agent), each party receives the copy signed by the other. Until contracts are exchanged, either party can withdraw from the transaction without penalty. It is only once contracts are exchanged that you have to move forward (think of this as the tearing-the-tag-off-the-new-designer-jacket moment). In the case of the buyer having a cooling-off period, the buyer is not bound to continue until the cooling-off period expires, but a break fee may be payable.

7. Payment of deposit

The deposit (or deposit bond, underwritten by guarantee) must be paid on or before contracts are exchanged. The deposit paid can vary and is normally paid to the real estate agent, who holds it in trust pending completion. It is normal practice for consent to be handed over at completion so that the agent can account to the seller. Until the deposit has cleared, the seller can rescind the contract at any time.

8. Cooling-off period

Depending on which state/territory you're in, a cooling-off period may automatically apply. Regardless of whether it's a standard inclusion, it can be added, deleted, shortened or extended, depending on your requirements, provided both parties agree.

There is no cooling-off period if the property is sold at public auction or on the day a property was listed for auction, and in some states, a penalty fee applies.

9. Insurance
The seller must take care of the property up until completion and the property should be handed over at completion in the same condition, subject to fair wear and tear, as it was at the date of exchange. If the property is substantially damaged before completion, the purchaser has a right to rescind and have the deposit refunded, as long as they do so within 28 days of becoming aware of the damage.

If the damage is not substantial, then the purchaser may choose to move ahead with the purchase subject to an adjustment of the sale price to account for the cost of repairs. It's in these instances that a good lawyer is worth their weight in gold!

10. Transfer/stamp duty
Transfer/stamp duty is payable by the purchaser to the state government at the time of settlement and is calculated on the sale price. The higher the price, the higher the duty. Payment must be made before completion if you are borrowing money and, in any event, within three months of the date of the contract. Many first home buyer schemes waive this fee, which can be a huge win.

11. Council rates, water rates, strata levies
The contract provides that all rates and service fees must be adjusted between the vendor and purchaser at the settlement date. They are adjusted as if the rates are paid in full regardless of whether they are in fact paid or not, so it's worth using your solicitor to review council records, strata levy receipts and water usage and adjust accordingly to ensure that any outstanding liabilities up until settlement are paid from the sale proceeds

(to translate: get your solicitor to ensure any outstanding bills from before your settlement date will come out of the vendor's money).

12. Pre-settlement inspection

As a purchaser, you are entitled to – and should absolutely, without fail, complete – a pre-settlement final inspection of the property before you make the final payment and take occupancy. Once settlement takes place, it is too late to be finding that some of the inclusions are missing or that something has been damaged. It is extremely difficult to get repairs done or inclusions returned after settlement is completed. For buyer protection, this is ideally done immediately before the settlement, however, practically speaking it's often done up to 48 hours prior.

13. Readying for settlement

In the week before you are due to settle, you should ensure your lender is ready to transfer the final monies required. These days, with instant online bank transfers, it's usually pretty straight-forward, though it always pays to check in. If you're moving into your new pad immediately (congrats!), book your removalist and make a list of the places you need to advise of your change of address, so you can do this soon as settlement takes place. It's also worth considering putting on a postal redirect to catch any you may have forgotten. Don't do it before, just in case there is a delay in the settlement. And, of course, don't forget to switch over your utilities (including internet connection).

14. Settlement

At settlement, the deeds to the property are handed over for payment of the sale price. If you feel the settlement date is not convenient to you, talk with your solicitor/conveyancer about it before exchanging contracts, as this can't be changed later.

If the buyer delays settlement, they will normally have to pay compensation to the vendor – not an extra cost that you want to incur!

The time of day that settlement happens is determined by the availability of all parties, and is usually managed online through a series of processes as managed by the solicitor/conveyancer (legal) and lender/broker (finance).

15. After settlement

Immediately following settlement, the real estate agent will be given authority to release any keys to the buyer, granting them access to the premises. Time to attach that fancy keepsake keyring to your new house keys!

During the week after settlement, your solicitor/conveyancer will send you final letters of confirmation of your purchase together with final statements and any other documents they hold. You won't receive a Certificate of Title (Title Deed) if you have a home loan, because all title documents are retained by your lender who will register the transfer into your name at the Land Titles Office, as well as advise a 'Notice of Sale' to notify council, the water authority and valuer general of the change in ownership so that all future rate notices are issued in your name.

16. Moving in

It's normal that occupation of the property is not granted until after the settlement has been completed, unless some other arrangement is made. You should not assume that the seller will allow you to move in before settlement, even if the property is empty. Because you may not have a firm time and date for settlement when you want to book the removalist, it is difficult to organise the removalist to arrive and load your old place and manage to arrive at your new property to coincide after the settlement time.

It's worth putting a plan in place that works around these issues, such as paying an extra day's rent for the removalist to hold your goods overnight, or trying to negotiate schedules between all parties.

17. Buying with an existing tenant

If a tenant occupies the property and they have a current lease, then you take over the vendor's role as landlord immediately after settlement occurs. The current lease remains in force and as the new landlord, you are bound by the terms of that lease. If you want the tenant to vacate the property, you will need to serve a notice of termination that adheres to the required period of time in accordance with the contract and laws.

When the tenant remains in the property, the rent needs to be adjusted and, if paid in advance, the seller will credit you in the settlement. If the rent is in arrears, no adjustment is made as the purchaser is not expected to take over a debt that is owed to the prior owner. Any issue here is strictly between the tenant and the vendor.

Quite often the adjustment of rent will be made by the managing agent as they often collect rents weekly, but account monthly to the landlord, so they could be holding rents in their trust account. Your solicitor/conveyancer will figure out what and how adjustments are made.

18. Ongoing costs and responsibilities

Now that you're a proud homeowner (yay!), your responsibilities have just begun. As well as your mortgage, you'll be paying rates, utilities and, where applicable, other levies and taxes.

First things first, you'll want to get your place insured. Your lender will have made the loan conditional on this.

At the end of the financial year, you may be taxed – for instance, holiday and investment homes in NSW may be liable for land tax.

As an investor, you may also be eligible to claim tax deductions for maintenance, improvements and if your place is negatively geared. As with all your finances, keep good records and consider engaging a professional to assist. Ensure you're planning and budgeting ahead to cover all upcoming costs and review regularly to ensure you're making the most of any opportunities to reduce them.

Yours for the win

Phew, that was quite the rundown ... If it all feels a little over-whelming, don't panic! In the next chapter, I'll introduce you to your dream team – the people who can help you through each of these steps.

But more than anything, I hope this chapter sparked your awareness that finding a way into property ownership has many different pathways. Doing your research, opening your mind to opportunities and creating them by getting out there and meeting people may be the key to your property dreams.

● ● ● ● ● ●

ELLEN, 30 – VIC

My fiancee and I are rentvesters with two investment properties and we are currently considering purchasing a third. We are Melbourne-based, and when we first looked at buying around the area we wanted to live in, we could only afford an apartment or a small older home that would need a lot of work. So we invested interstate instead.

We used a property investment company to help us purchase and build our two properties. We wanted to purchase land and this company aligned with our values. We did not have the knowledge or time to research and find the perfect area to invest. Although we did pay a fee for this service, I think a decision to purchase the wrong property in the wrong area had the potential to be significantly more costly.

Both properties are growing in value and are in areas where rental vacancy rates are 1 per cent. We were able to use some equity from our first purchase for the second house and will be able to solely use equity for the third. I'm super passionate about rentvesting and love that you guys are sharing that this is an option!

● ● ● ● ● ●

TAKE NOTE

Buying a house today requires a significant portion of your income, can take years to save a deposit for, and even then, can remain far out of reach.

....

The state and federal governments support several schemes to help first home buyers get a foothold into the property market. Those that don't qualify for these opportunities still have options if they're prepared to think outside the box and consider approaches such as co-ownership, tiny homes and rentvesting.

....

Once you're ready to purchase, you'll go through a series of stages to complete the purchase. There are several professions available to assist you through these, which we'll go through next.

....

Chapter 5
Assembling your dream team

Over the last few chapters, I've given you a bunch of pretty serious things to think about before leaping into buying a property, so if you're starting to feel a little, perhaps *a lot*, overwhelmed, I don't blame you! Perhaps go for a quick run around the block – I'll be here waiting when you get back to introduce you to all the wonderful people who will make proceeding with property-buying a piece of cake.

The good news is that there are plenty of real-time, full-time, fully qualified professionals ready and waiting to give you all the support and advice you need. Some won't even cost you a cent.

Of course, the usual caveats apply – you need to scope them out properly and make sure the advice they're offering is actually what you need and what you're willing to pay for. Surprisingly, some of the cheapest advice may be the best. (Also, it may be the worst.) So how do you figure out who you need on your team and who to stay clear of? Let's run through the types of professionals you might like to get onboard and consider how to pick the best person for you in each category. Then you can decide if they're good enough to join the elite crowd you're running on your queenly way to home ownership.

KEY TERMS

buyer's agent: professional who finds and negotiates property sales on behalf of the buyer.

conveyancer/solicitor: a legal professional trained and qualified to handle the transfer of real estate from one person to another.

estate: the legal term for everything you own.

family: either your best or worst friends on the property-buying journey – all depends!

guarantor: becomes legally responsible for paying back your loan if the borrower cannot.

pets: always welcome, at least in my house!

selling agent/real estate agent: professional who sells properties on behalf of a seller (vendor).

vendor: the owner who's selling their property.

bank/lender: the institution you'll set up your home loan (mortgage) with.

mortgage broker: works their relationships with a variety of lenders to get you the best home loan deal.

People you don't need

Let's get the people you *don't need* out of the way. Usually, god love 'em, it's friends and family, with the odd real estate hound thrown in.

Friends and family

I hate to break it to your Uncle Richard, but just because he bought a house in the 70s doesn't make him the most qualified person to help you. Likewise, your parents and other extended family members may not have a clear picture of the market right now, or just how much things have changed since they were last actively in the game.

A selling agent

When it comes to *buying* property, a selling agent is not on your team. In fairness, their role is to represent the seller and get them the best possible price for their house while meeting their other key objectives like, 'I want out of this place ASAP. I've just left my husband and a new life awaits! In circumstances like that, the sales agent will be as equally invested as the seller in finding a committed buyer who can move quickly.

If you've spent some time building up relationships with the local sales agents and they know that you're ready to jump on the right place and have your finance all set, then guess who's the first person they'll call? You, that's who – and if you're real lucky, before the place even gets listed.

But even in these situations, stay alert. Until you've exchanged contracts, a professional real estate agent will always be looking to land the best deal for their client. Just make sure it works for you too, and everyone's a winner.

While sales agents will (probably) never be your best mate, it's worth maintaining this relationship into the future. When you're renovating, they can be a great sounding board to ensure you're investing your money into features that will appeal to the market, and when it comes time to sell, you'll already have someone you can trust to work with.

The media

For the most part, the media loooove to sensationalise and dramatise what's going on in the world. To make the day's events 'newsworthy' they like to find an angle that will tickle your not-so-funny bone. Often that means over- or under-reporting on the real impact of things like interest rate rises, property prices and building failures, among other things. So, sure, while I always agree that it's important you do your research and get informed, also take the 'news' with a grain of salt and be wary of the source of your information. Ideally, run cross-checks that take a variety of positions, or better still, investigate the actual data. If that all sounds boring, find someone – or a group of someones – whose voice, information and knowledge is credible and whom you trust.

People you do need

While most of the people in this chapter you might be able to take or leave, these are the professionals who form the core of your property dream team. It's pretty unlikely you'll be able to pull off a smooth and smart property purchase without them. So, if money's tight, if nothing else, at least budget for these services – and, as always, shop around to get the best price for the best provider, #moneywin.

Lender/mortgage broker

Without doubt, you'll need a lender – in other words, a bank (unless that uncle of yours comes to the party with his cheque-book). While you can go direct to a bank and sign up for a mortgage, it often pays to engage a mortgage broker.

What's the difference? A bank/lender is the institution you'll set up your loan with. A mortgage broker has relationships with several of these, so the idea is they can look around on your behalf and get you the best deal.

Because of Australia's financial laws, mortgage brokers are not allowed to charge you money for securing your loan. They make their money from bank commissions, which they have to declare. You get full disclosure on the fees they earn, so it's all above board, and working with them won't cost you a cent. Sure, they're incentivised to secure you a loan (they won't get paid otherwise), but that's pretty much your key objective too, right? They're also obliged to advise you of the risks of borrowing too much, and you can ask them to run several scenarios until you land on one that works for you. Basically, your success is their success.

Where a good mortgage broker can be invaluable is that they work with a wide variety of banks and lenders and will search for the best loan for your needs and circumstances. That includes being able to access interest rates that are generally not available to the public, not only saving you time, but also saving you real money. Because they have professional connections with several lenders, they're generally able to get you a better deal than if you go directly to a single bank. Think of it like shopping for a jumper – you could just go to Country Road, or you could access all of Westfield to get the best deal.

On the flipside, when a lazy mortgage broker comes to town, they might try to railroad you into a loan that's easy for them. Frankly, it's pretty obvious when this happens, but make sure you keep your eyes and ears open. If your broker starts insisting that you have to sign up with a partner even though you explicitly stated you were doing this on your own, or only ever offers you one bank lender when you've asked for several, or keeps directing you to buy a house and land package in a suburb you've never heard of . . . run. It shouldn't go that way and if it starts to, there's something very wrong with the picture.

How does it work?

When you first meet, your broker (or lender) should spend a decent amount of time finding out all the things that are important to you in the way you want the loan structured, such as being allowed to pay it down every week, or whether you expect to pay it out early, or because you're a savings diva, you have an account for every budget and want each one to contribute to your offset account.

From there, a great mortgage broker (hello, Zella Money! All shameless plugs here) will hunt around to find you several options they'll review with you. They'll take time to discuss each one's pros and cons and how they may affect you both now and down the line. For example, one might have the lowest interest rate, but no flexibility and a huge early-exit penalty, where another might insist on a higher deposit, but allow you to split your loan.

It may very much feel right now as if you'll *never* be able to pull a deposit together, but the good news is that a decent mortgage broker will also look at your personal situation and direct you to all the ways in which you might be able to access various supports such as first home buyer schemes, or your super, to help you reach your dream. That's why, even if the reality of buying a home might feel a very long way off, it could be worth speaking to a mortgage broker today, so you can start figuring out your options and creating a strategy that works for you.

In either case, whether you go directly with a lender or use a broker, you'll want to engage with them as soon as you start seriously looking to buy. They'll get you to the stage of pre-approval, which is a non-guaranteed offer to loan you a specific amount of money. With this in hand, you can go to inspections and start making offers, feeling confident you can fund your decision.

Building, pest and strata inspectors

The last thing you want once you finally settle on your dream property is a nasty surprise, whether that be an insect infestation or significant water damage. A combined pest and building inspection can give you peace of mind that you're making a (structurally) sound decision and give you the full picture of what repairs and maintenance you may need to factor in once you own the property.

The building inspector will write up a report summarising the property's condition. The report will include notes of any problems, such as safety hazards, leaks, and any structural faults, such as issues with the roof or add-on extensions. Ideally, you'll want to meet the inspector onsite and walk through the property with them. That way they – and you – can point out any concerns and have them looked at in detail. While you might panic that a bowed floor in a heritage home means expensive restumping in the future, an experienced builder will be able to tell you if it's standard wear-and-tear that, while not looking great, has no significant impact. At least, that's what happened to me when I bought my first place. (Thanks, Bill, I appreciate you more than you know.)

Likewise, with a pest inspection. I don't know about you, but I like to steer as clear as possible of furry creatures with long tails and other almost-invisible creepy crawlies. Pest inspectors, on the other hand, love unearthing them. And while I never want them in my house, I'd prefer if an expert found them *before* I signed on to own a menagerie, rather than having to replace termite-infested roof beams less than two months after I've moved in. Sadly, that happens more than it should, so it definitely pays to get a keen eye looking around on your behalf and steering you well clear of that particular disaster.

Engaging these inspections, often combined as a two-in-one visit, will not only save you from potential trouble, but if they locate repairable damage, you could use their notes to negotiate a better deal on the house.

It's worth keeping in mind that there are some things a building inspector won't include in a report, because they don't deal with every aspect of a property. Also, if furniture and other things are in the way, or if they deem the roof or underfloor access too tight, they won't inspect there. Because of this, they won't necessarily include everything in the written report either, which is another good reason to walk around with them. If you're lucky and they're a qualified builder who regularly works on the tools, they may even be able to give you a rough guide as to the costs of any improvements or repairs, none of which will be included in the report.

Hot tip: If some unforeseen issues do arise down the track, you'll have much better luck claiming on your insurance if you can show that you took all reasonable precautions to avoid the problem.

Additionally, if you buy into a strata (unit, flat, apartment), you will want to inspect, not just the building, but its management and operations. The strata management takes care of the building and grounds, pooling residents' funds for insurance and maintenance. Engaging either your solicitor or a professional firm to review the body corporate reports will give you a clearer view on the current state of the building and any potential upcoming major works or defects that you might need to fund, reviewing things such as:

● What insurances are in place.
● What the quarterly levies are.
● What the financial position of the scheme is.
● If there are any ongoing maintenance problems.
● If there are any special levies struck for the cost of any works to be done.
● Any other matters that may be reported in the records or minutes of meetings.

Legal professional – solicitor or conveyancer

A legal professional is essential in the home-buying process. They review the contract to ensure there are no hidden nasties and ensure a smooth settlement. While you may think this is something you could do yourself, a well-trained professional eye can save you a LOT of headaches. Your legal team has the experience to know what to look for in a contract, and the tools and systems to help facilitate an easy-breezy transfer of the ownership, including registering the title in your name and ensuring that the seller has discharged all their outstanding liabilities on the property. Much of this process is done online now using special keys and certified IDs that must be registered through select portals as part of the process, so it really is quite difficult to do on your own.

When it comes to buying and selling property, you can either engage a conveyancer (a licensed professional who specialises in processing property sales) or a solicitor (a qualified lawyer, ideally with expertise in property). Many local law firms will offer conveyancing services for a set fee which can be comparable to standalone conveyancers, anywhere from $400 to $2,500 depending on the complexity, so it definitely pays to shop around – standard practice for SOTM devotees, of course!

Who you end up choosing mostly depends on what you're looking for – the right combination of price, convenience and service. A conveyancer processes property sales for a living, so they will ensure a standard sale runs smoothly. However, if you need to consider the long-term implications of how the ownership structure may affect your business or loved ones, then a lawyer who also specialises in corporate structures and/or estate planning may be a better option.

Additionally, if something goes wrong, lawyers can engage at a level beyond what conveyancers are qualified for. While standard issues can be dealt with as routine by either party, resolving tricky issues that pop up at your settlement inspection, or negotiating complex changes to the contract including addendums and caveats, requires a firm hand and someone who's confident to engage in legal bravado. The best of both worlds could be in a law firm with an in-house conveyancer. This gives them access to a trusted team and the appropriate services as and when they need them.

YOUR DREAM TEAM

PEOPLE YOU DON'T NEED	PEOPLE YOU DO NEED	PEOPLE YOU MIGHT NEED	SUGAR ON TOP
FAMILY & FRIENDS * SELLING AGENT THE MEDIA	LENDER/MORTGAGE BROKER BUILDING/PEST INSPECTOR LEGAL PROFESSIONAL	FAMILY & FRIENDS * ACCOUNTANT ESTATE PLANNING LAWYER	FINANCIAL ADVISOR BUYER'S AGENT PROPERTY MANAGER

*DEPENDS!

People you might need

These professionals are definitely worth considering, depending on your personal circumstances.

Friends and family

Yes, yes, I know what I said before. BUT ... the *right people* among your friends and family could be a stellar choice to add to your crew, if:

They're your sibling who's at a similar life stage to you and is also (or has recently been) hunting for their first home. In that case, they could offer a trusted ear and accompany you to inspections to be your sanity check and sounding board. Someone needs to be sure you're actually sticking to your non-negotiables and not buckling weak-kneed at the first sign of a sunlit studio painted fresh in your favourite colour (to hide the cracks, no doubt). Their job is to point out that, while it's a neon-pink, subway-tiled delight, the bathroom is also leaking water and, by the way, there's not actually enough room in the 'master bedroom' to swing a cat, let alone fit a double bed.

They're your parents and they're willing to help you out financially. I know not everyone has access to the Bank of Mum and Dad, but is there a chance a family member could help out by going guarantor? Perhaps . . . although, this is not something either of you should enter into lightly. A guarantor becomes legally responsible for paying back your loan if you, the borrower, cannot. If you don't have enough of a deposit, or your lender isn't confident in your ability to repay a loan, they may ask for a guarantor. In many cases, guarantors use their own property as security against the loan, which means if something happens in the market that puts your place at risk, it might affect your family home's security too. Do you really want to be responsible for putting your folks out on the street in their old age?

They're your friend who knows you best and can ask you the tough questions along the way. As with your sibling, if your mate is travelling the same road, they could be a great sounding board and sense-check on the reality of your choices. Since you turn to your friends for advice on other big life events, like your career or your personal life, it makes sense to talk about your property dreams with them. But be cautious, particularly if your friends don't share your property values. Take your friends' well-intended advice the same way you should eat tomatoes – with a pinch of salt.

They're someone who's walked the walk. While we all know how annoying well-meaning-but-unasked-for advice can be, if it's *you* who's prompting the conversation, you may unearth some real gems over work drinks, a neighbourhood barbecue or Sunday brunch. Getting amongst it is a great way to educate yourself. The more aware you become of how the property market operates, the more you can fine-tune your personal strategy for navigating it.

These convos don't have to get deeply personal, but it can be refreshing to hear others' takes on what's happening in the local area and real estate in general. Likewise, listening to podcasts, reading books or joining communities like our She's on the Money and The Property Playbook Facebook groups. These spaces are filled with others just like you, sharing relevant tips and wisdom.

Of course, being the savvy SOTM-er I know you are, you totally get that the info nuggets you pick up this way are general in nature and not specific to your own personal circumstance. Remember: with every piece of advice you hear, check back in against your own goals and values – all that fabulous work you did in the early chapters – to ensure that whatever pearls of wisdom you choose to keep are the right fit for you.

Accountant

The role of an accountant is to help to manage your finances and tax obligations, so they can be very helpful when it comes to buying a home. Often, they will already be looking after your mandatory financial paperwork and reporting, so they may be cheaper to engage than a financial adviser. Unless your situation is quite complex, or you want one-on-one direction with long-range goal setting (that's where financial advisors come in), an accountant can help you with much of the practical side of managing your budgets, cash flow and reporting.

Accountants are also invaluable in helping guide your structural decisions. While you'll need a lawyer to arrange the paperwork, your accountant can offer advice and direction on the impacts of the various ownership structures available. They'll also look at the effects of the money flow from an inheritance perspective – otherwise known as 'estate planning'. As this can all get quite complicated, it is definitely worth engaging a professional to discuss it with you in detail. In these scenarios, your dream team would include a lawyer and an accountant that you engage to speak directly with one another and yourself to work out the optimal solution from both a legal and financial perspective. Once you've determined a plan, you'll have some specific guidelines for your loan structure to bring to your lender/broker.

Estate planning lawyer

Research from Finder Australia in 2022 found that 60 per cent of Australians don't have a will.[31] While none of us likes to think about it, you don't want all your good gear distributed to the mean girls just because you didn't commit your post-life plans to paper. If you've put a significant amount of effort into building a decent life – and let's face it, if you're Team SOTM and reading this book, then I'm pretty sure you have – you want to be certain that everything you worked hard to gain won't be shared in ways you're not happy with.

If you fell into a coma yesterday, what would happen to all the hard work you've put in up until now? Do you have a plan in place for who will manage your affairs in the event you become incapacitated and inherit your assets if the worst comes to pass? If not, you should, or you're at risk of Aunt May swooping in and claiming everything for herself, simply because you wrote her a note in Year 3 promising her your Barbie collection.

In truth, a scrap of paper like that – no matter how pretty the sparkly pen you used – would hardly stand up in court. But if there's nothing else to go on because you haven't laid out your wishes in a clear, verified manner, there's no telling what could happen.

Let's put it another way. If you're lying there in permanent dream-state, your closest family and loved ones will be dealing with so much stress and worry that the least you could have done was to plan in advance the ways in which they should deal with your stuff, so that's one less thing they have to worry about. Especially if that inheritance is a big fat load of old debt with a side portion of house.

When you purchase a property, you're taking on a significant asset/liability. And that comes with a lot of responsibility, even after you're not around to see it. It sounds morbid, but it's so important that you have the conversation and prioritise making a plan.

A good and clear legal document – a will – makes a big difference. It directs how and to whom your estate is divided. It's for that reason I'm including an estate planning lawyer in this chapter, a professional who specialises in this area. If you've chosen to work with a legal firm for your conveyancing, they'll have someone there who can help you with this – estate planning. This same person can talk you through how best to structure your property's ownership in the first place, to ensure that what you hope for in your will is able to be enacted. Many people don't realise that legal structures trump desires, so it pays to have everything working in alignment.

Insurance broker

If the worst thing happened to you yesterday, would you be prepared? If you have insurance, the answer is yes – financially prepared, at least. When you're a homeowner, there are a few types of insurance you should consider taking out. Just as a mortgage broker can help you find a great deal on a home loan, an insurance broker can help coordinate a set of policies to cover your needs.

There are several types of insurance you might need. Home or building insurance will be required by your lender, but those covering your income and personal circumstances are up to you. We will go into all of these in much greater depth in Chapter 11. For now, briefly, the types of insurance you might consider include:

● home insurance
● contents insurance
● landlord's insurance
● income protection insurance
● life and critical illness/accident insurances.

Sugar on top

This category is for professionals who definitely aren't essential, but are worth considering to make your property journey a little bit easier (and less stressful).

Financial adviser

A financial adviser's role is to help you set up and keep track of your financial goals. Initially, they will spend a good amount of time reviewing your current and projected income and spending, including things like whether you might be hoping to take time off for family planning or sabbaticals, spending on investments and guilty pleasures and finding ways to do both healthily, setting aside money for tax obligations and taking you right through to how you'd like to pass on your inheritance.

As such, they will have a solid view of all aspects of your financial and life goals and can help you decide if the property you have in mind is right for your budget and suits your goals. Together with your accountant, they can also guide you in deciding which property ownership structure might work best for you now and down the line – and believe me, this can get a whole lot more complicated than you could ever imagine (more on that in Chapter 6).

In Australia, it's mandatory for financial advisers to be licensed. They have to have attained a minimum of a bachelor's degree and must also pass the financial adviser exam to attain their licence plus complete continuing professional development in order to retain it, so the advice they offer comes from an expert's position.[32] That said, they offer a range of services at a range of prices, from the bare basics of budgeting right through to complex structures and estate planning.

In an ideal world, you would work with a financial planner who is comfortable and supportive of investing in both shares and property. In the real world, they'll often favour one or the other, with many of their fee structures tied to the kind of services they're offering. Some may charge you a percentage of the value of the portfolio they manage on your behalf – similar to fund managers – while others may charge by the hour, and others still, a set fee for service. Depending on the level of service you're accessing, this can add up, and it's quite possible that much of the support you need, at least in the early days of your wealth creation, can be managed by your accountant.

Buyer's agent

Think of a buyer's agent as the opposite of a selling agent – they are paid to advocate on your behalf and search for the best property for you. They come at a significant cost, but the upfront outlay could result in a good deal.

Generally, buyer's agents' fees begin at around 2 to 3 per cent of the purchase price, in addition to GST and an engagement fee to get started.

Having a buyer's agent in your corner means you have an all-round property buying expert on hand. They are usually total pros in negotiating a great price, so they could save you money and then some, even accounting for their fees. If you opt to rentvest in another state, for example, a buyer's agent could hunt down the perfect property on your behalf and, more importantly, run the numbers from a yield/growth perspective to ensure it meets your goals.

Property manager

This applies to those who are purchasing an investment property. A property manager is the go-between for tenants and you, the owner. They are responsible for finding new tenants, checking references, collecting rent, booking repairs and conducting inspections to help maintain the overall standard of the property.

Fees vary like any professional service, but it is usually between 7 and 10 per cent of weekly rental income. It may be expensive to hire a property manager, but they can save you a lot of time and energy when it comes to looking after a rental. Remember how I wrote about the importance of taking the emotion out of a property when rentvesting? Well, that is exactly what a property manager can do.

● ●

ASSEMBLING YOUR DREAM TEAM

Now that we're up to speed with the different types of people out there who can help, consider these questions:

1. Who might you add to your personal dream team in terms of roles?
2. Do you have anyone specific in mind who might fit any of these?
3. If not, how might you go about finding and assessing who would be a good fit?
4. When might you start getting in touch?
5. Can you make a SOTM action plan to help you create your contact list?

....

....

....

....

....

● ●

NICOLE, 30 – ACT

I purchased my own apartment in May 2020, having just turned 27. So many people were saying the world would implode and not to go making risky decisions like buying property, but it was the best decision I ever made. The whole thing was kind of an accident . . . I didn't even have pre-approval on a mortgage! I'd been living downstairs for the past two years and stumbled across the home when it was open for inspection.

My parents have never had a mortgage or debt (they purchased their house for $50,000 cash in regional NSW in 1987 and have paid cash for second-hand cars). We had one house, one car as a family of four and Mum (nurse and breadwinner) and Dad (teacher) both worked. This meant I had nobody to help me understand anything about mortgages, useful debt, the processes etc.

Luckily, I had an excellent neighbour who was crucial in helping me feel okay with a mountain of debt and gave me a bunch of tips on how to be smart about it. I had lots of conversations with my friends (many of the older ones who had more knowledge of the property game) to get suggestions on mortgage brokers, lawyers etc. I've always tried to be quite transparent with my financial situation as a single woman – to both give and take knowledge. I also got onto educating myself, then helped my sister buy a property 18 months later with her own mortgage!

When I bought, I took advantage of the first home buyers grant, which meant no stamp duty or LMI. This was a huge help. I did a building inspection because I noticed some cracks in the walls (my lack of building knowledge had me concerned this was a huge red flag . . . turns out it wasn't), but it also highlighted a small amount of moisture in one location I hadn't been aware of. The inspection 100 per cent put my mind at ease going into the property. I would pay the couple of hundred dollars to do that again for sure.

In 2022, I relocated to Melbourne for work. I was planning on having my dad be the property manager and deal with everything because I didn't want to pay for a real estate agent. However, in the end I shopped around and landed a good deal with the folks who sold me my apartment to manage it. It's another decision I'm so glad I made and means I don't have anywhere near the stress I could have had, plus I get freedom in my life. It also means there's

*no tension between Dad and me about property/business matters
(another win!).*

*All in all, listening to my own instinct as well as including the right
people along the way (while ignoring the wrong ones) has made my
property journey a breeze.*

● ● ● ● ● ●

TAKE NOTE

Buying property is a long, detailed process. Even when
it's rushed, it always pays to know who to trust.

....

It can be easy to be led astray – no-one is an expert in
everything. That's why it's so important to engage the
right professionals to assist. It might seem like an added
expense, but it's one worth its weight in gold. Even Baby
needed Johnny in her corner (and to pull her out of it).

....

When it comes to property, you need a trusty
little black book. Start yours, stat!

....

Chapter 6

Getting your finances in order

So, you've found a home you love and you're ready to buy! Or are you?

To make an offer on a house, you need to know you can afford it and for this you'll need a loan. Or at least, conditional pre-approval of a loan.

So, do you run straight to your nearest bank? Not necessarily. While the Big Four (ANZ, CBA, NAB and Westpac) sing their loans all over the internet, there are many more options available, with a whole host of smaller lenders out there who just may have a package that suits you better.

That's why I recommend sitting down with a mortgage broker who will look around on your behalf and pull together some options that should best suit your circumstances. Also, rather nicely, they will sit down and explain the whole process – not just the loan schtick, but the inside-out on property and how it works, far better than any website can.

In this chapter we'll go through the steps and processes of securing a home loan in detail.

KEY TERMS

30-year term: the term of your mortgage (or any contract) is how long it will last. If you exit the term early, there may be penalty fees.

ADI – Authorised Deposit Taking Institution: the industry term for what we call banks and credit unions, regulated by APRA in accordance with the Banking Act.

APRA – Australian Prudential Regulation Authority: an independent statutory authority that supervises institutions across banking, insurance and superannuation, and is part of the federal Department of Treasury.

ASIC – Australian Securities and Investments Commission: an independent Australian government commission that acts as the national corporate regulator in areas of financial services and consumer credit.

bank/lender: though we often think it's a 'bank' that must loan us money to buy property, there are several types of financiers who can assist you with this. We use the term 'lender' to cover them all.

Big Four (the): the four major consumer banks in Australia: ANZ, CBA, NAB and Westpac.

conditional pre-approval: conditional (not guaranteed) approval of the amount a bank/lender is willing to lend you for a home loan, based on their assessment of your income and spending and the type of property you're looking to buy. The exact figure (and unconditional approval) is generally only available once the actual property you're wanting to buy has been bank valued.

default: the technical term for missing a mortgage repayment. Not something you want to do if you can help it, my friend, as it comes with a bunch of penalties.

good debt: debt used to help you get ahead in life, so something I consider worth carrying – such as a loan for a home or education.

HECS/HELP debt: a loan from the Australian government for tertiary education. While interest free, it is indexed to inflation – meaning that each year, student loans increase by the rate of inflation. At June 2023, this was 7.1 per cent.[33]

interest-only loan: a loan where you pay only the interest on your loan for a set period of time. When you're paying interest only, you're not paying down any of the principal of your loan.

investor loans: loans for properties that will be rented out. These usually attract a higher interest rate.

LVR – loan-value ratio: before confirming your loan, your lender will get your property independently valued to assess its worth. This helps determine how much they'll lend you, based on the LVR, i.e. how much you're borrowing against how much the property is worth. Your LVR affects whether your deposit savings are enough to waive LMI.

non-bank lenders: in addition to ADIs, money-market dealers, finance companies and securitisers are also authorised to loan money.

owner-occupier mortgage: a mortgage for a home you will live in, i.e. as an 'owner-occupier'. These form the majority of the mortgages taken out by the SOTM community.

principal-and-interest (P&I) loan: 'principal' is the amount you borrow, 'interest' is the fee you're charged for doing so (usually a percentage of the principal) and a P&I loan is when you pay back both.

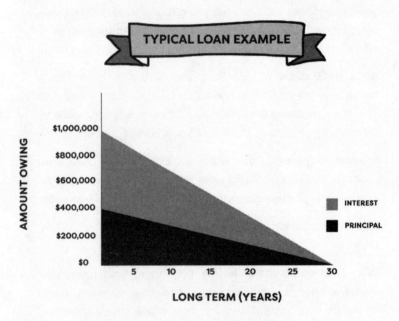

TYPICAL LOAN EXAMPLE

Difference between 'principal-and-interest' versus 'interest-only' loans

Who will lend me money to buy a house?

If your goal is to buy a property, the first thing you need to know is how much you can spend without over-stretching. The best way to do that is talk to someone in the know. So, what are your options?

Mortgage brokers

Brokers facilitate the lending process. They will do some research on your behalf to determine which lender can offer you a loan that suits your needs and budget and which government assistance schemes you may be eligible for. (For more details on how brokers work, flip back to Chapter 5).

Of course, I love my mortgage-broking business, Zella Money, as it's run by a team of millennials who understand you and the space you're playing in, and I'll take any chance to spruik them! But as long as you're working with someone who's looking out for your best interests and who you trust, they could be a great addition to your property dream team.

Banks and credit unions

Most people looking to buy a house will borrow money through a major bank like ANZ, CBA, NAB or Westpac. Known as the Big Four, these banks service around three-quarters of home loans for owner-occupier mortgages. If you're using a broker, it's likely that they will have a strong relationship with one or more of them. But there are almost 100 banks and nearly 40 credit unions and building societies registered as ADIs in Australia, all regulated by our prudential body, APRA.[34] Most of them have home loans on offer, so keep your options open. Professionals in certain industries (teachers, nurses, police, etc.) may have associated credit unions that can give them a good deal, so if that's you, be sure to look into what's available to you.

Non-bank lenders

Money-market dealers, finance companies and securitisers are also authorised to loan money and are regulated by ASIC. Driven mostly by mortgage lending, this sector is growing in Australia and is currently around 5 per cent of the market. While the RBA identifies these lenders as riskier since 'a greater share of their lending is to borrowers who are self-employed or employed in industries more sensitive to economic conditions, and who have low levels of documentation',[35] independent risk assessor, Moody's Analytics, reports that non-bank mortgages have performed well over recent years and loss rates have been low.[36] In other words, if you are struggling to get finance with the major banks, these lenders could be an option. Just ensure you read and understand the fine print.

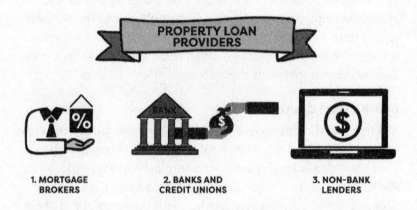

PROPERTY LOAN PROVIDERS

1. MORTGAGE BROKERS

2. BANKS AND CREDIT UNIONS

3. NON-BANK LENDERS

Who to choose?

The good news is that in Australia, both banks and non-bank lenders are carefully regulated. This means your money is protected by ASIC and the National Credit Code.

Each institution will offer different things, so it really depends on what you need and what you are looking for. As you'll have heard me say many times, it always pays to shop around. It's usually a trade-off between a competitive interest rate versus flexibility, which we'll go into a little further below. Non-bank lenders can offer similar features to banks, such as offset accounts, because they usually team up with another bank to help fund investments.

As with every step of the home-buying process, once you've made a shortlist, it's worth going over everything again in fine detail before signing on the dotted line for your chosen loan. It costs money to get into and out of loan arrangements, so be sure you know what you're agreeing to and how much it might cost.

What your lender/mortgage broker is looking for

In order to qualify for a home loan, there are a few things a lender is looking for. At your first appointment with your mortgage broker or lender, they will ask you to bring some documents so they can assess where you stand. Much like a first date, you want to make yourself as attractive as possible. Unlike a first date, this has less to do with hair and make-up and more to do with a good-looking portfolio of solid financial health. Though that sure is sexy too, if you ask me!

What to bring to your first meeting:

- Bank statements showing your earning, spending and savings.
- Balances on all credit cards and any other loans or post-pay credit facilities.
- Pay slips proving your income.
- Tax returns.
- A list of assets (shares, cars, jewellery and other valuables).
- Your budgeting spreadsheet.

The above is just a general guide and will differ depending on the lender and financial situation.[37] During the loan application process, each of these is assessed in order to determine your eligibility for a loan and how much you can borrow. In order to present yourself in the best light, here are some things to keep in mind. As some of these take time to get together or prove, it's worth getting them sorted well before it comes to loan application time.

Banking on your budget

The bank will look very closely at your earning and spending habits. While you will submit a budget spreadsheet, this will be reviewed against the actual monies incoming and outgoing through your bank account(s). While some of this assessment may be automated, anything that causes concern will be highlighted for manual review. This is why I don't recommend using 'fun' descriptions on your money transfers – lines like 'drug money' may be funny to those who know you personally, but they are an instant red flag inside the banking system.

Savings are queen

As mentioned, you will need a deposit before you can apply for a mortgage. What's more, the bank will prefer to see that you have been able to save and build this over time, rather than it arriving suddenly in one lump sum just prior to submission. Lenders like to see that you are capable of living off your earnings and saving money simultaneously. (Lucky we're good at multitasking!)

Something to consider when it comes to deposits: even if you don't qualify for one of the government schemes that allow you to take a loan with a less than 20 per cent deposit and no LMI (remember we discussed these back in Chapter 4?), you may well decide, after discussing the pros and cons with your accountant and/or broker, that proceeding with a smaller deposit (and accepting the LMI) is preferable to waiting. The way Australian property prices tend to increase, this can often work out to be more affordable.

A question of credit

I often get asked by the SOTM community about credit cards when it comes time to applying for a home loan. In the USA, showing a healthy ability to pay off your credit card each month can add positively to your credit rating, which can help your loan application. In Australia, however, your credit cards are not reviewed for this purpose.

If you have a credit card or have ever applied for a credit or loan, you can access your credit score instantly online at financial comparison site Canstar, that uses Equifax's rating (one of three agencies in Australia) to give you a credit score between 0 and 1200.[38] There is no minimum credit score to get a loan in Australia, but banks like to see evidence of paying off debt in full and on time. This includes utility and service bills, so get in the habit of paying these before they fall due. Late payments will reflect poorly on your credit score whereas paying in full and on time works in your favour.

When applying for a loan in Australia, your credit card limit will be considered as debt you are carrying (yes, even if you pay it off each month in full and it has $0 balance when you apply). Missing repayments or juggling debt between several cards can be seen as negative behaviour. (And no, despite persistent rumours, checking your credit score does not affect your credit score.) This is often why your mortgage broker may suggest you close your credit card and other loan and post-pay facilities (Afterpay, Zip Pay and the like).

Hot tip: The limit you're carrying on each line of credit reduces the amount you can borrow for your home loan. If you're a savvy SOTM credit card user and pay off your balance in full each month, essentially using your card for the loyalty points and insurance it offers, you may not want or need to close it completely. Instead, reduce your credit limit for the period in which you're applying for loans.

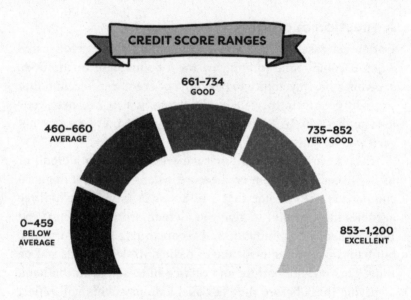

(Source: Equifax[39])

Pre- and post-pay instant cash

You may want to close down all your pre- and post-pay lines of instant credit before you apply for a loan. While they seem appealing with no upfront costs and interest rates, the penalty rates that apply if you miss your payment deadlines are relatively harsh.

Unlike credit cards, which can offer some advantages, as listed above, unless you really need an instant fix that you know you can absolutely close out within the payment timeframe, then signing up can be a very slippery slope to a debt balloon. This is the worst money habit to fall into.

Proof of income

If you have regular employment, this will be your pay slips. If you work in the gig economy, the need to prove a regular income can be the most difficult hurdle you'll encounter when applying for a home loan. While it's still possible to get a home loan with casual employment, it is important to understand that lenders are strict on the terms of your income due to the responsible lending requirements outlined by the National Consumer Credit Protection Regulations.

Lenders typically want to see that you've been receiving a reliable income from a regular source for a minimum of six months. If you work several jobs to earn your keep, having an accountant on your team will be invaluable, to help you gather proof. Your business accounts and tax returns will be vital here.

If you are considering changing careers or jobs, keep this in mind, too. Starting out on a new career path is less desirable from a lender's point of view. Moving employers but remaining in the same industry is considered a safer bet (though that may still come with the uncertainty of a six-month probationary period). If buying a home is your priority, maybe save that career change until after you have secured a property.

Dependants

Same goes for family planning. If you don't have dependants, a lender will look more favourably on your application. Those little cabbage-patch dreams of yours will cost somewhere between $160,000 to $500,000 to look after until age 18, and the banks know it![40]

If your dreams include buying a house and starting a family, maybe try to plan for it in that order. (Buy now, baby later.) Again, with the right mortgage broker, this may be less of an issue, so don't be disheartened if you're already living your best-parent life. As we know from Chapter 4, there are support schemes in place for single parents too.

What about my HECS/HELP debt?

HECS/HELP debt lives in the category I like to call 'good debt'. Like a home loan, because your debt has been accrued to help you get ahead in life, it's something I count as a worthwhile investment.

That said, there's no denying it is still debt, and your lender will count it as such. So, should you pay off your HECS/HELP loan before saving for a house deposit? That's most definitely a conversation worth having with your accountant. Again, like LMI, if acquiring property is your long-term goal, it may some-times be a smart move to live with it in order to outrun Australia's historically rapidly rising house prices. Alternatively, the very bitey indexation that's been applied to our HECS/HELP debts recently is nothing to be sniffed at.

All I can say for certain is that this debt will be counted in your liabilities when it comes to applying for a home loan. For some, if your HECS/HELP debt continues to increase, it may become a genuine roadblock to you being able to access other credit down the line.

● ●

YOUR FINANCIAL GLOW-UP

Review each of the criteria a lender will look at when considering your loan application (credit score, income, assets, liabilities, budget, etc.). In which areas could you give yourself a financial glow-up?

....

....

....

....

Consider using some of these approaches:

1. Create a budget and cash-flow system (without restricting
    yourself – we're just using it as a tool to see what comes in and
    what goes out!).
2. Review your budget to see where you could cut things out in
    the short term to turbocharge your savings and help you in the
    long term.
3. Review all your personal debts and smash them down. Start
    with the debts that have the highest interest rates and work
    your way down.
4. Negotiate, negotiate, negotiate! Whether it's hustling down
    your phone bill, reaching out to companies you have debts
    with to see if they'll work with you, or asking your boss for a
    raise – negotiating is one of the tools you're going to need for a
    financial glow-up AND to land your dream property.
5. Try to stay focused on the outcome. Sometimes the journey
    can be overwhelming, so keep your original vision front of mind,
    to maintain your motivation.

....

....

....

....

....

● ●

How much money do I really need?

Back in Chapter 3, I outlined various strategies to help you move past the apparent barrier to saving for a deposit and helped you properly account for a property's purchasing costs. As this sample table shows, there are many additional 'hidden' costs that come into play when buying a home, that are worth keeping in mind as you prepare your 'true cost' of home ownership. To keep things straightforward here, I've only shown the example that includes all potential costs, including LMI and stamp duty, which may be waived if you secure a first home buyer grant. When it comes time, make sure you get exact prices from your providers. Let's go through each of these in detail.

Purchase price	**$500,000**
Stamp duty (non-first home buyer)	$8,750
Building/pest inspection	$600
Mortgage registration fee	$187
Transfer fee	$1,120
Loan application fee	$600
LMI (with only 10% deposit)	$12,000
Council and water rates	$500
Conveyancing and legal fees	$1,800
TOTAL hidden costs	**$25,557**
TOTAL COSTS to purchase house	**$525,557**

Transfer (stamp) duty

Transfer duty, also known as stamp duty, is a one-off tax levied by all Australian states and territories on property purchases. The amount differs from state to state and can be based on the property purchase price, location and property purpose (business or residential). Some states also charge different rates for investment properties versus places of residence.

Similar to the tax system, the rate of stamp duty progressively increases in brackets. For example, in Queensland, purchases up to $5,000 attract no tax at all, similar to the tax-free threshold. Purchases between $5,000 and $75,000 are taxed at $1.50 per $100, those between $75,000 and $540,000 at $1,050 plus $3.50 per $100 and so on, gradually increasing to the upper limit of $38,025 plus $5.75 per $100 for properties over $1 million. Rates and brackets vary quite a bit between states, so check with your state or territory for exactly what you'll be up for.

With the median capital city house price in Australia at June 2023 sitting at $869,666,[41] it's easy to see how you'll typically pay tens of thousands in transfer duty when you purchase a property. Most first home buyer schemes waive or reduce this fee, depending on the purchase price.

Transfer duty may be charged on any property transfer from one party to another, including to those who may inherit your property later, depending how the estate is willed. This is one reason to look more deeply into your ownership structure and estate planning (which we'll check out in detail in the next chapter).

Document transfer and title registration costs

These are government fees applied to each document that is lodged for registration on the property title. Typically, there is one transfer document and one mortgage document that you'll need to pay for at the time of settlement.

Council and water rates

Council and water rates are adjusted between the vendor and purchaser as at the settlement date. They are adjusted as if the rates are paid in full, regardless of whether they are in fact paid or not. Any outstanding rates are paid from the sale proceeds (being the vendor's money), while the buyer takes ownership of rates from the date of settlement.

Legal and conveyancing fee

This is a service fee you pay for a legal professional to transfer the property into your name. You could technically save money by doing it yourself; however, if something went wrong in the process, it's not a risk I would personally be willing to take. Conveyancing fees vary, and it's worth getting quotes to compare how much you are likely to pay, as they can range from $400 to $1,800.

Loan application and service fees

Your lender will usually charge you a fee for processing your loan application. You should also factor in ongoing fees for servicing your home loan. Even if it's just $10 a month, this could add up to thousands of dollars over the lifespan of your mortgage.

Mortgage establishment fee

These are the fees a bank or lender charges to establish the mortgage, often in addition to your loan application fee, covering such things as the bank's legal fees as well as settlement fees. This usually covers the bank's valuation of the property too.

Canstar's mortgage calculators show lender's fees range from less than $100 to upwards of $900, depending on the category and the lender. If a lender is offering a great deal on interest, it's worth reviewing the fees they're otherwise charging.

Lender's mortgage insurance (LMI)

As we've noted, if you have less than a 20 per cent deposit, lenders will typically charge you LMI to cover the insurance against their risk of taking you on as a client. This is based on your loan–value ratio (LVR) – the ratio of deposit you are putting up against the total value of the loan.

For example, if you were purchasing a house for $600,000 with a deposit of $30,000, you'd be looking at a lender's mortgage insurance fee of around $20,000, according to Westpac's online

LMI calculator.[42] However, as discussed earlier, Australia's competitive housing market may mean you're better off paying this, to get in earlier. Only you – in consultation with your dream team – can decide which option works best for you.

Additional costs

In addition to fees identified as part of the property purchase, Canstar also recognises three other important costs to keep in mind:[43]

● Home and contents insurance
● Moving costs
● Utility and services connections.

Your real budget

Once you factor in the additional costs to purchasing property, for a $500,000 property, according to Realestate.com.au, it will cost you somewhere between an extra $16,000 for first home buyers (waiving transfer duty), or an extra $26,000 for non-first home buyers. However, including the additional costs suggested above and if the purchase price is higher, Canstar suggests these extra fees could be as much as $40,000.[44]

It's important to factor these costs in when considering your budget. If, for example, you have been pre-approved for $500,000, taking these additional costs into consideration, in actual fact you have $484,000 as a first home buyer or $474,000 as a non-first home buyer to spend on the property itself. Keep this in mind while house-hunting – you don't want to find yourself caught short by thousands of dollars!

Even more importantly, if you're 'lucky' your lender may offer to loan you more money than you thought you needed or could afford. While it might be tempting to take as much as they suggest, it is so important for you to have done your own sums factoring in variations on interest rates, your changing financial circumstances and life plans (are you planning any time off working in the future?) and the management costs of property ownership.

If you're not sure of these yet, don't worry, we go through many of these in Chapter 10. But let this be a big sign from your She's on the Money fairy godmother, saying: Please don't be tempted by things you can't afford. Most especially, shiny pretty home loans that could trip you up if they're simply too big and not the right fit for your bright, dreamy future.

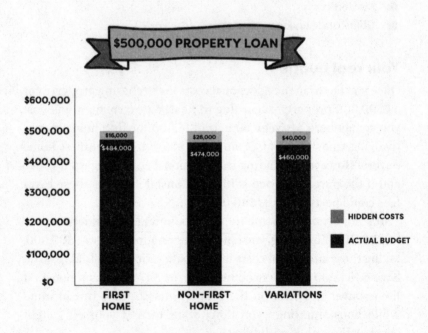

Your real property budget

ESTIMATE YOUR COSTS

Purchase price	
Stamp duty	
Building/pest inspection	
Mortgage registration fee	
Transfer fee	
Loan application fee	
Lender's mortgage insurance	
Council and water rates	
Conveyancing and legal fees	
Home and contents insurance	
Moving costs	
Connection fees	
SUB TOTAL hidden costs	
TOTAL COSTS to purchase house	

Accessing government grants

Home buyer assistance grants (see Chapter 4 and appendix) can only be accessed via authorised participating lenders. Each lender is allocated a set number of grants at the start of each financial year and once their allocation is exhausted, borrowers have to wait until the next release.[45] In that way, I guess comparable to trying to get Taylor Swift tickets . . . though somewhat more likely. Applications can only be made with a participating lender or their authorised representative (a mortgage broker), not directly with the government body managing the program.

The advantage to accessing these programs is that, for the most part:

- Your transfer (stamp) duty is waived, saving you around $8,750 on a $500,000 home.
- You could secure a loan with as little as 2 per cent deposit (with the rest guaranteed by the scheme).
- You should be offered competitive interest rates equal to someone securing their loan with a 20 per cent deposit.

There are several eligibility requirements to accessing and using these schemes. If you're interested in determining which, if any, of the home buyer assistance schemes may suit you, it's best to discuss this with your mortgage broker in consultation with a participating lender.

Conditional approval

Before a lender offers you a loan, they will review your capacity to service (pay off) your mortgage, then evaluate your deposit against the property's value, to determine the risk they are taking on and how much they are prepared to loan you (calculating your LVR).

All of this takes time, so it's worth undertaking the process at the same time as you are actively looking to buy, in order to secure loan pre-approval, aka, conditional approval. If you are pre-approved for a loan, this means that a lender has given you 'approval in principle' to borrow a certain amount, based on your serviceability.

When applying for conditional approval, the lender will ask:

● the price range of properties you're interested in
● how much of your deposit you have saved
● your income
● your living expenses.

Having this confirmation gives you and the real estate agent confidence that you're in a position to move quickly to purchase a property. This is critical if you are bidding at auction, as there is no cooling-off period, so if you're forced to rescind your offer due to lack of finance, you will lose your 10 per cent deposit to the vendor as compensation (ouch!).

Having pre-approval can be equally valuable in the highly competitive major cities' markets, as knowing you have the funds available means you're in a position to attach a cooling-off waiver, which could put you at an advantage when negotiating.

If you're early on in your home-buying journey, getting conditional pre-approval can help you focus your property search by giving you a clear idea of what you're likely to be able to afford, based on what a lender is prepared to loan you.

If something changes while you're looking for a new home – your financial situation, for example – you must get your conditional pre-approval reviewed.

Your deposit

'Victoria, until now you've always suggested a 20 per cent deposit?'

Ah, yes. This is a rough guide. From a lender's point of view, they prefer you to have 20 per cent of the house price saved, to meet the industry-standard LVR of 80 per cent – making you a safer risk, and so you can avoid paying LMI. But as you've seen, this amount can vary. Using the support of home-buyer schemes, the deposit your lender requires can be reduced to as low as 2 per cent.

Likewise, the deposit required by a property sales contract also differs. Property contracts may only require 10 per cent of the house price. That is what we're looking at now, the deposit you pay upon exchanging contracts, to secure the property. Whether or not the bank requires you to put forward 2 or 20 per cent of the deposit has nothing to do with how much the property sales contract requires you to pay on exchange.

So, how and when do I pay the deposit?

Once you find a property that you're keen to buy, you should simultaneously have the property sales contract reviewed by your solicitor and notify your lender. The lender can review your pre-approval in line with the property you are considering, to make sure their offer and loan amount still stands, often pending a valuation.

It can be a whirlwind from the moment you make an offer, to having it accepted and exchanging contracts, so you want to be sure you have everything at the ready to ensure a smooth process. In order to exchange contracts, you will need to return your signed copy of the contract, along with your deposit. Although, verbally, you and the vendor may have agreed on terms, until the deposit clears, the vendor may rescind their agreement.

Normally you will be asked to pay your deposit into the real estate agent's trust account. These days, it can be an almost instant transaction using online money transfers, assuming you have clearance from the bank to process the full amount. If you have multiple signatories on the account or a funds transfer limit, this may hold up the process, so it's worth checking with the bank prior, to ensure you have everything in order.

Once your deposit arrives to the real estate's trust account, these funds cannot be released unless agreed to by both parties, which makes them visible and accessible, but keeps them safe until the matter proceeds to settlement. Once you have exchanged contracts, you are liable to execute the agreement as stated in the contract, including settling on the date specified in the contract.

Establishing your loan

On settlement day, you will have to pay the balance of the sale price and any additional costs from the lender and services. Between exchange and settlement you will finalise your loan agreement, in order to ensure there are funds available. During this time, the bank will get your property valued by an independent valuer, which, together with your deposit, will determine your LVR and help to finalise the loan offer. There are several parameters the lender will use to adjust their loan offer. The three most important are:

1. Usage: owner-occupier or investor

One of the drawbacks of rentvesting is that a lender will classify you as an investor (unless you live in the place for at least six months initially, to qualify for first home buyers' schemes and owner-occupier capital gains tax reductions). This classification will affect both the amount of money they're willing to loan you (often less), as well as the interest rate they offer (often more).

2. Interest rates

These are mostly what affects your serviceability over the long term. When you decide on what mortgage structure you want, you have three main choices: variable, fixed, or split.

Variable loan

A variable loan is when the interest rate changes over time depending on the rate the lender sets, which is generally led by the RBA's cash rate rises or cuts (which is why these cause such a flurry in the news). This means that the amount you pay towards your mortgage can fluctuate over time, depending on market conditions. There is less certainty for a variable loan, so it can seem like a trickier option, but it's worth keeping in mind that there are pros and cons to both a variable loan and a fixed loan.

Pros of a variable loan

- Lenders, in general, offer competitive rates.
- You can have access to extra features, like offset and redraw accounts (more on that soon!).
- You're not penalised for paying off your loan sooner.

Cons of a variable loan

- It's trickier to budget and plan, because the amount you pay changes over time.

Fixed loan

If you opt for a fixed loan, you can fix your interest rate for a set period of time, such as five years at 5 per cent. Once this chunk of time is over, the loan then reverts to the current variable interest rate.

Pros of a fixed loan

- Your repayments stay the same for the duration of your fixed loan rate, a win for budgeting simplicity.
- It may cost you less in the long-run, depending on various loan features.

Cons of a fixed loan
- If interest rates go down, you're stuck paying a higher amount.
- You may incur significant 'break costs' if you choose to refinance your loan before the end of the fixed term.
- They don't allow for additional repayments, which limits your ability to pay off your loan more quickly.

Split loan
A hybrid of both worlds. You can slice up your mortgage and have one part as a fixed loan and the other as a variable. It doesn't have to be a 50/50 split, you can also split into multiple fixed (maybe one three year and one five year) and one variable loan. Your lender/ broker can help you to find a combination that works for you.

Pros of a split loan
- You get the flexibility of a variable and the stability of a fixed home loan.
- You could have access to features not available on fixed-only loans.

Cons of a split loan
- A split loan may not be offered by every lender, restricting your options.
- The lender may place restrictions on the features of the loan which may not be present on a variable-only loan.
- When interest rates change, so too do the repayments for the variable portion of the loan.

3. Repayment terms
Here your lender is most interested (ha, no pun intended) in whether you are looking to pay back both your principal and interest, (P&I), or interest only.

Principal and interest (P&I)

Unless you have a lot of room to manoeuvre, this is the more likely. You'll be paying off the principal – the amount of debt you are paying back – as well as the interest – what the bank charges you for the loan, as a percentage of your loan.

Think of interest as the 'rent' for the money you're borrowing. As we now know, interest rates are impacted by the market, as well as the RBA's official cash rate. The cash rate is the amount that banks pay to borrow money from other banks in the money market. Therefore, the bank passes this cost on to their customers who borrow money. At the time of writing, the official cash rate is 4.1 per cent. In home loan terms, that's translating to around 5.9 per cent in fixed mortgage rates and closer to 6.3 per cent at the variable rate.

Interest-only loan

This is a loan where you pay interest only for a set period of time. You don't need to pay any amount towards the principal. It sounds great, because the repayments are smaller, but interest rates tend to be higher for these types of loans, according to Canstar.[46] So, it's not all good news and you could end up paying more than you need throughout the life of your mortgage.

Also, for as long as you're paying interest only, you're not paying down any of the money you've borrowed from the bank, which essentially means you're not getting ahead. Investors use this funding type as a way to secure and service loans in the short term, since they will pay off the entire loan with the monies earned from selling the property.

Loan duration and repayment schedule

Property loans are generally set to a standard 30-year repayment term which is designed to suit family home buyers, but not so much the investor. As touched on earlier, lenders make money charging for ongoing loan services and annual fees, so it's worth their while to keep you over the long term. As such, loans often come with a penalty fee for terminating early – including if you simply want to refinance to access a better rate. They may also limit your ability to make additional repayments. Both these restrictions tend to apply to fixed-term loans, which also generally offer lower interest rates.

Facilities

While this is not something the lender cares so much about, for us SOTM budgeting bosses, cash flow is queen. Many in our community like to keep track of their budgeting using several bank accounts allocated to each money bucket. If this is you, looking into which facilities your lender offers in conjunction with your loan will be super important.

Offset account

An offset account is a normal bank account that's linked to your mortgage. What's great about an offset account is that any amount of money in it reduces the amount of interest you have to pay on your loan. Say, for example, your home loan is $600,000 and you have $10,000 in your offset account. You only have to pay interest on $590,000. The amount you pay per month per your repayment rate won't change (unless you're on interest-only), but you will be paying off your loan faster.

Redraw

A redraw account is another nifty feature. Essentially, any additional payments you make on top of your minimum repayments contribute to an amount of cash you could redraw. There is a big BUT here: depending on the terms and conditions of the account, there could be fees and a waiting period before you receive your funds, as well as limits on the number of times you can withdraw money.

YOUR LOAN REQUIREMENTS

Reflecting on the variety of features your property loan could include, as outlined above, list the ones most important to you.

....

....

....

Loan approved

Once your loan is approved – and generally it won't be formalised until you have decided on the property, had an offer accepted, and a bank valuation is completed – your lender will process the necessary paperwork to put the loan in place. Whose name the property will be registered in becomes important here, so we'll get into that in the next chapter. And if you're now wondering why and how you can manage the steps involved in securing both a property and a loan to cover it, don't stress yet – I'll run through all that in more detail in Chapter 9.

● ● ● ● ● ●

RACH, 27 – SA

We bought in December 2020. My partner already owned a home, so we decided to sell that one, which raised half of the deposit we needed for our new one.

My partner had built that house and I had never been in the property market before, so it was interesting talking about our priorities. As he wasn't interested in building again, he wanted a house with a nice kitchen and bathrooms and a decent backyard for a dog. I was willing to go for a fixer upper and didn't mind too much about the size of the backyard. I was keen for wooden floors because I was over having tiles and carpet.

The one thing really that we were inextricably aligned on was budget. When we went to the broker, I was shocked – and I mean SHOCKED – by how much money the banks were willing to loan us. Luckily, we'd already had the discussion and decided on our ideal price and absolute limit. I really think this helped us not get distracted by the *shiny* seven-figure loan we were offered. For context, the number we signed up for was about half that.

After sending each other what felt like thousands of property listing links and viewing nearly as many places, we finally settled on a consolidated list of priorities.

1. Keeping to our budget
2. Property size >500sqm
3. Location within a 10 km radius of the city.

By shedding our 'cosmetic' expectations and approaching anything that suited our criteria with an open mind, we finally found the house of our (at least for now) dreams.

CASEY, 24 – QLD

My partner and I bought a house together in October last year. He contributed more to the deposit than me and my income is about half of what his income is.

We put down $100,000 towards a deposit – he paid $55,000 and I paid $45,000. We wanted to help free my weekly cash flow a little bit because I am earning less, so ultimately, we decided to contribute the same percentages to the mortgage repayments as we did for the deposit. I pay 45 per cent and he pays 55 per cent. If we ever need to sell, this is how we will split the property's profits too.

If we make any improvements or renovations, we will also split the costs for this in the same way. Our shared bills are based on our earnings too, and have an equitable split, so I can afford to save money.

TAKE NOTE

While you can go direct to any lender, it may help to work with a mortgage broker. They will be paid by commission from the lender, so it won't cost you upfront.

....

Give yourself a financial glow-up (get your savings in order, clear your credit card debt, etc.) to ensure you meet all the important criteria a lender will consider when reviewing your application.

....

The purchase price is only part of your loan. Take into account all the fees, charges, insurances and duties you will need to pay before you can call the property yours.

....

Being clear on your immediate and long-term goals and repayment strategy will help ensure you establish a loan facility that suits your needs.

....

Chapter 7

Structures and planning

There's a lot to think about when buying a home, but I'm guessing that a property's title isn't the first thing on your mind. Perhaps you're not even sure what that means! All will become clear.

There are quite a few types available, so it pays to know what you're getting into. In this chapter, we take a detailed look at the types of properties and ownership structures available.

Confusingly, the way the government describes 'property types', in terms of grant eligibility, is different from how they will be listed on a property contract. In the case of the property title itself, this is simply how the property is registered with the state land and titles office. You won't get any say in this, but it will affect how you can use the property and various associated costs.

I'll also get into the nitty gritty of some legal stuff when it comes to property ownership. It's so easy to get caught up in the excitement of the process, but taking the time to understand the potential long-term impacts of your choice of ownership structure is critical.

KEY TERMS

community title: similar to strata except that maintenance is typically handled by the property owners and upkeep is managed by a residence committee.

estate planning: estate planning is a fancy way of describing the ways in which you want your affairs managed and your possessions dispersed after you die.

joint tenants: 50/50 property ownership between owners with right of survivorship.

land title registry: the land registry in each state/territory maintains the register of land titles and manages the transfer of titles under their domain.

leasehold titles: instead of buying a property outright, you purchase a long-term lease. This is commonly found in government- or church-held properties.

negative gearing: when your investment property costs you more to run than the income it generates. This loss can be used to offset your taxable income.

SMSF – self-managed super fund: a super fund you manage yourself (with the help of financial professionals, ideally) that requires costly audits and reporting. Not something I suggest for the SOTM community as a general rule.

sole ownership: a property is owned by one person.

strata title: the usual type of title for apartments and flats, as well as many retail shops, offices and most townhouses.

tenants in common: property ownership split according to agreement, with the right to will your portion to your nominated beneficiary.

Torrens title: freehold title of land which may have a free-standing or semi-detached house on it. It is wholly owned by the property title holder.

● ●

MAKE A PINTEREST BOARD

Learning about these things can be a bit dry, so I like to imagine how each of these looks while I'm learning about them. (I'm a definitely visual learner!) If you're anything like me, maybe you could start a Pinterest board and collect examples of each type of property as you're learning about them.

● ●

Types of properties

The way properties are marketed is often quite different from the way in which they are legally registered. This section goes through the main types of properties as they appear when listed for sale. The terms here are useful for anyone looking to buy and also align with the descriptions used by the first home buyer schemes.

An existing house, townhouse or apartment

This is exactly what it sounds like – an established property that is already built and technically ready to live in straight away. It may be brand-new or it may be a century-old grand dame, so its condition could affect your 'real' ability to be able to move in immediately. If it's older and a bit run-down, that may increase its affordability, but you may also need to do some work on it to make it habitable. Remember that although your property contract includes the buildings or lot on title, it doesn't cover the condition of the buildings. You may have heard the saying that property is sold *caveat emptor*: buyer beware.

A house and land package

A house and land package is when a parcel of land and a home design is packaged up in one process, but with two contracts in place: one directly with the builder and one with the developer. Typically, the project is managed through a central supplier – your project manager – who deals with council approvals and coordinates the purchase-to-build process. This option can be a simple and cost-effective way for prospective homeowners working to a tight budget to get a foothold in property while building a house that suits their specifications. Generally, the design choices, inclusions and add-ons are laid out so you can pick and choose what suits you. We'll cover the pros and cons of this approach to buying in Chapter 8.

Land

This option puts you in the driver's seat and gives you the most flexibility, as you are responsible for the design, construction and budget of your house. It may also be risky, as building costs and labour availability are more of an unknown and can escalate.

If you are in the enviable position of having more money to spend, you may be better off splitting your land and construction. Since the first home buyer schemes place upper limits on the purchase price, you could direct the concessions to the land purchase price alone, if it's a more expensive area. However, you will need to ensure you can then afford to build a home on top of this.

An off-the-plan apartment or townhouse

This is when you buy an apartment or townhouse that has been approved for development but has not yet completed construction.

Buying this way often means you can purchase below market value (compared with completed places in the same area with similar attributes) and can choose the design finishes (often you'll get a choice from a limited set of colours and finishes). If you choose this option, make sure you are confident in the reputation and performance of the developer. Much of the discount comes from the risk you take on in committing to an unfinished product.

Types of property titles by law

While it may be easier to think about your property types as described above, that's not how they appear in your sale contract. Each property type has an impact on your overall costs, legal considerations and buying process. The main types of property titles in Australia are as follows.

Torrens (Old Systems or Limited) – freehold titles

When you purchase a house on its own block of land, it typically falls under a Torrens title, or freehold title. In the 2021 Census, this type of property accounted for 73 per cent of land holdings in Australia, so they are by far the most common.[47] Occasionally, the outmoded title types – Old Systems or Limited, both of which existed prior to Torrens – will pop up, but all are freehold; meaning that the owner has full control over both the land and buildings on the title. It's worth noting that most semi-detached houses (semis), despite sharing a common wall, are on Torrens title.

Strata (Company) – lots titles

Strata title is the most common form of ownership for apartments and flats, as well as many retail shops, offices and most town-houses. Introduced to replace the previous Company title system (mostly outmoded, but still found in a few older buildings), strata titles were established as means of controlling ownership of parts of a building, known as 'lots'. In strata title, people own their apartment individually and share ownership of common spaces like external walls and windows, hallways, lifts, stairs, driveways, gardens and recreational facilities. Owners pay quarterly fees and special levies to the strata scheme to cover expenses associated with common property maintenance, building insurance, finances, by-laws and more.

Community titles

Community titles are similar to strata titles in that they involve regular management payments, ownership of lots, common property spaces, by-laws and owners' corporations. Where they differ is in the way they're managed. In community title arrangements, the maintenance is typically handled by the property owners and upkeep is managed by a residence committee. While local councils may provide some services, it's often limited, so the community scheme is usually responsible for managing its own garbage collection, gardens and roads. For this reason, community titles generally apply to large developments and gated estates, so they're much less common than strata schemes.

Leasehold titles

Leasehold titles most commonly apply to government-owned or church-owned land, which is then leased instead of sold. Unlike typical rental leases, under leasehold titles the lessee can lease the property for up to 99 years. Instead of paying to purchase the property, you pay an initial cost to set up the leasehold – often, but not always, less than a Torrens title in the same area – as well as annual rental payments.

TORRENS   STRATA   COMMUNITY   LEASEHOLD

Different types of property ownership

When it comes time to buy, your lawyer will ask you whose name should appear on the contract. Sounds straightforward, right? Not always. There are several ways to structure the ownership of a property, which can become increasingly complex if you're looking at directing inheritance and limiting liability and tax burdens.

You have options to consider when deciding upon the legal owner of a property. This becomes especially relevant when it comes to selling the property, and even more crucial when a person named on the property title dies. Yes, I know in this loved-up phase of building our lives and futures, that's probably the last thing you want to think about! But it's important. If you're dancing on the other side of the rainbow, you don't want your loved ones squabbling over a house.

For real-life help with this stuff, your trusted accountant and lawyers are the team to turn to. They can offer advice and help set up anything you might need. Just remember, though, the more complicated and sexy a plan sounds, the more expensive it will be to set up and manage. Think carefully about how important the structure really is, and whether you actually need that level of complexity in your life, or if a more straightforward approach could do the trick.

That said, it is critical that you do understand all your options and the effects of these decisions down the line. It's not enough to have a verbal agreement with your co-owning mate as to who will take out the bins and what you'll do if one of you can't make their mortgage payment that month. These decisions not only need to be talked through, but legally written up (well, maybe not the bins, but definitely the repayments). Your ownership title will go some way to this, but you may need addendums to your contract to ensure you're covered for the important situations.

So, let's go through the major options available in terms of property ownership. While, I don't suggest that these are all suitable for first home buyers, in the interest of giving you the full picture, here they all are.

Sole ownership

This is a simple one – it means the property is owned by one person. A single person's name – a real person, not a company or trust – appears on the property title. If this is you, congratulations!

Joint tenants

After sole ownership, this can be the most straightforward structure if your priority is to ensure a direct transfer of ownership to your spouse in the event of your passing. When parties own property as joint tenants, all tenants have shared ownership and interest in the property and a right of survivorship exists. That means if one of you died yesterday, the other would automatically own the remaining share of the property.

It also means each owner has an even split of the property's profits, losses and risks – in other words, anyone listed on the title is responsible for paying the mortgage has an equal share in any income if it's a rental and can be sued for damages should something go wrong with the place. (Did someone say insurance?)

In some states, joint tenancy is the default ownership structure if buying as spouses, but since the introduction of capital gains tax in 1985, a tenants in common arrangement might be better suited, particularly for investment properties as this allows more flexibility when assigning property title in ways that can reduce the tax burden.[48]

Tenants in common

In my business, Zella Money, I'm seeing an increase in friends or relatives buying houses together. In this case, you'd want to consider a tenants in common arrangement, whereby two or more people co-own the same property, but with no right of survivorship.

Unlike with joint tenancy, the portion you hold under a tenancy in common is 'willable' by you to a beneficiary under your will or certain persons where you have not made a will. With this arrangement, your friend or spouse could leave their share of the property to their mother instead of it reverting automatically to you.

The other benefit to this structure is that the ownership allocations and responsibilities can be split however you decide. It could be split 50/50, like a joint tenancy, but you could also split it any number of ways, depending on the amount each person puts in and how many of you there are, say 70/30, 60/40, or even 10/10/10/5/3/2/10/10/10/10/10/10 if you wanted to get really crazy.

How you choose to split may depend on the initial deposit each owner contributes or represent planned repayments over the long term or any other way that's agreed. Once set, the ownership split defines how the property's profits, losses and risks are divided. That said, certain agreements, such as those with your lender, will insist on treating all owners as both collectively and individually responsible for fees and taxes so, as always, be aware of the fine print.

Company and trusts

Using a trust as an ownership structure means that you won't be the investment property's legal owner, but rather, the beneficial owner. This means that the trustee (which can be an individual or a company entity) will own the property. This may not be an accessible or necessary option for everyone, particularly a first home buyer, but it comes up, particularly when people start talking investment properties plural.

Whether you establish a company or trust depends on the purpose. Yes, my friend, we're back to the strategy table again – c'mon, this is (debatably) more fun than Monopoly! The main reason investors choose a trust for their property purchase is to create separation between the asset owner and those who will benefit from it. The advantages of this include asset protection, tax planning and estate planning purposes. Effectively, the control of the trust can be transferred without incurring capital gains tax or transfer duty – so long as ownership stays in the trust.

A trust deed prescribes exactly how the trust will operate and each party's role in the trust: a settlor, who sets it up; a trustee, who owns the property; and a beneficiary, who the trust is set up for. Trusts are often used in family properties, like large estates or farms, as the inheritance can transfer down the family line with no capital gains or duty transfer tax impacts on the beneficiaries – so long as ownership stays in the trust.

Be careful if you're planning on using a trust to manage your investment property. Any costs for maintaining the investment property are recorded in the trust and cannot be used to lower your personal tax bill.

Self-managed superannuation funds

While some may suggest buying property (or other investments) through a self-managed super fund (SMSF), it comes with several restrictions, including not being allowed to be used (either lived in or rented) by the fund member or any of the fund members'

related parties (meaning no relatives, children or business partners). If bought through an SMSF, the property must solely be
used for investment purposes only – in other words, at very, very
arm's length.

Purchasing investments through your SMSF comes with so
many handcuffs, along with the already onerous complexities,
reporting requirements and costs of managing the fund, that I
don't think it's an option that would be the right fit for many in
the SOTM tribe. Personally, I feel they don't offer enough benefits to outweigh the complexity and cost of managing them . . .
but if they float your boat, please look into them.

Why do we need to nominate how we hold the property?

Remember back in the last chapter we mentioned that your
lender will need to know whose name is on the title? The tenancy
nominated is recorded on the document lodged at the state land
and titles office and subsequently on the new Certificate of Title.

- Your bank will need to know how you hold the property, in
  case of default. If the property is held as tenants in common,
  depending on how the mortgage is registered, the bank may
  only be able to claim the portion related to the defaulting
  party.
- If one party dies, a Notice of Death is completed and lodged
  at your state's land and titles office. If you hold a joint tenancy
  and mortgage over a property, it is a much simpler process to
  have the property transferred to the surviving person. If the
  property is held as tenants in common and each party holds a
  mortgage with a different bank, and one party has died and
  willed their share to a 'new' person, this can be a complicated
  and lengthy process.
- Your state revenue office needs to know how you hold a
  property. If you own more than one property, you may be

liable to pay land tax, calculated on the value of your land (not your house). Your principal place of residence is generally exempt from land tax, but check with your state revenue office for details.

● If your holding of the property is clear and you leave a valid will, then the distribution of the property (either by way of a transfer to beneficiaries or sale) should be pretty straightforward.

JOINT HOME OWNERSHIP

Estate planning and wills

Listen, I know you don't want to talk about this, but what kind of a financial adviser (retired or otherwise) would I be if I didn't at least get you thinking about some big, hairy, important life questions? If you are going to sign on for the biggest loan (and biggest dream) of your life, then you ought to consider planning for its biggest eventualities too.

At some point, we are all gonna leave this planet. That's a fact. So it's important to get organised. These queries are certain to pop up during the 'who shall we put down as the owner on title' convos anyway, so you may as well start thinking about them now. Since your lawyer and accountant will be sorting various things for you on these fronts already, let's get them to set up and/or review your estate plan, will and insurances while they're at it.

'What do you mean by estate planning, Victoria?'

Estate planning is just a fancy way of describing the ways in which you want your affairs managed and your possessions taken care of should you become unable, through incapacitation or death, to care for them yourself. Naturally, it's a subject that most don't like to think about, but you know what's cool about it? When done, it actually gives you HUGE peace of mind.

First, it puts you in charge of yourself, even when you are no longer capable of it. Your estate planning documents make your wishes clear, so those who may end up acting on your behalf will align with your intentions. It protects you, your assets and belongings and makes sure they're passed down to whomever you decide. And it also protects your family and loved ones who may need access to your investments to cover their living expenses. In a time of grief, this helps make managing your affairs as easy as possible.

While your 'last will and testament' is super useful, it's not the only thing that decides who inherits your OG Nike high-tops or half-paid-off first home. If you selected joint tenants ownership, then regardless of what your will says, your spouse will inherit your portion of your jointly owned house through the right of survivorship clause. Or if you are a tenant in common with six of your besties, you'd want to have written into your will who you'd like to pick up your seventh heaven, or it will be distributed to the beneficiaries of your estate as your executor sees fit.

Most people understand that your will specifies who (bene-ficiaries) should inherit your estate (assets – cash, property, vehicles, etc.). While it's important to outline how your assets will be distributed, it's equally important to cover how any debts will be resolved. You should also specify how and who should handle things in your absence, so your estate planning should include things like appointing an executor, powers of attorney and guardianship, organisational requests for your funeral, ownership of specific items or belongings and guardi-anship of your children if you have them.

Nominating the executor of the will is crucial – who's going to be that responsible friend who ensures that everything you wanted and planned for gets respected once you're not around to see to it yourself. An executor could be anyone you like – a family member, a friend, or even a professional, like an accountant or lawyer, if you choose.

Think about how you want to distribute your estate – what will the split be and how will it work? What structure do you want? Are you going to set up a trust to reduce some of the tax burden, or is that overkill for you? Talk to an accountant or legal professional about all the pros and cons.

If you have children, it's important to make a plan for them in the event that both parents are unable to care for them. You could choose anyone you like to take care of your kids; however, one thing that I always liked to remind my clients of is that the person who becomes responsible for your children doesn't have to be the same person who manages your assets for them. You may elect two separate people if that makes you feel more comfortable.

If someone dies without a will (dies 'intestate'), the court generally grants administration of their estate to the person or people with the greatest entitlement in the estate (this may be a spouse or children), or to the state public trustee service. If this is you, it's a lot to leave to chance. Do you really want to leave your loved ones with such a big legal and admin headache?

Making an estate plan

An effective estate plan will cover:

Naming your beneficiaries. These are the people to whom you gift your assets, which could include a continued income stream to reduce uncertainty in a time of great stress. The wishes in your estate plan are legally binding.

A minimisation of taxes. When planned properly in advance, your estate plan can be structured so that as little as possible of your estate is lost to taxes.

Putting all your affairs in order. As well as giving you peace of mind, having a certified will and estate documents reduces the chance that your family will have to deal with time-consuming and expensive administration processes.

Documents that you should consider drawing up include:

A will. Your will specifies your beneficiaries, assets and wishes, and nominates who you would like to administer this for you (an executor). While you can get a 'will kit' from your local post office, inheritance can be a lot more complicated than it first appears, so if you can afford it, it's definitely worth drawing up your will with a qualified lawyer who can explain all the ins and outs to you.

Power of attorney. Assigning a power of attorney gives a nominated person the authority to manage your financial affairs when you become unable to do so yourself. Trying to manage these without your written authority is almost impossible otherwise, so this is really important.

A living will. A living will details your wishes for the types of life-sustaining medical intervention you want or don't want, so that your wishes can be carried out if you are terminally ill or unable to communicate.

Enduring guardianship or healthcare proxy. In the event that you're unable to make these decisions for yourself, this authorises the person named, to make medical decisions on your behalf.

A trust. Depending on your situation and your assets, a trust may also be included in your estate plan or could even be the entity that holds title to your property, if that makes sense for your circumstances.

●●●●●●●●●●●●●●●●●●●●●●●●●●●●●●●

PLANNING YOUR ESTATE

Alright friend, it's time to get out your pen and ask yourself some hard questions. Who should inherit your assets? Have you got a will that details this? Do you have people appointed and structures in place to support this – an executor, power of attorney and enduring guardian? If not, it might be time to scout around for a trusted lawyer to help you.

●●●●●●●●●●●●●●●●●●●●●●●●●●●●●●●

Personal insurances

While you're having these conversations with your estate planning lawyer, they will likely bring up insurances. As dark as it sounds, in some ways, things are a lot more straightforward if you keel off the perch. While nothing will replace you or a loved one, life insurance can help ease your family's financial worries at this toughest of times.

On the other hand, if you're injured but unable to work, things can get complex and really challenging. If you're not earning an income, or it's been greatly reduced, this doesn't stop your mortgage repayments falling due. And being injured, it's very likely that your health bills and living costs will rise too. You can sometimes apply for a mortgage moratorium in certain circumstances, but even if you get one, it won't hold indefinitely. Eventually, if you can no longer afford your repayments, you may face the difficult option of having to sell.

This is where insurances really can save the day. Both income protection and TPD (total and permanent disability) insurances can cover any loss in earnings, so that you can continue to pay down your loan. Depending on your cover, you may even be able to pay off your mortgage entirely, which could relieve one major pressure and worry.

What insurances could you need?

Life insurance. This cover pays a lump sum in the event of your death. As a general rule, you should aim to have enough cover to pay all large debts and provide an additional amount that can be invested to earn an income to replace your lost earnings.

Trauma. Trauma or crisis cover provides a lump sum to help people recover from a traumatic event such as a heart attack, cancer or stroke. This cover can ease the financial stress of the medical incident and recovery, and is used for any necessary medical and therapy bills, home modifications or specialist equipment.

TPD. Total and permanent disability (TPD) cover pays a lump sum in the event you become totally and permanently disabled through illness or injury.

Income protection. Income protection can provide you with a safety net if you are unable to work in the event of a temporary disablement due to sickness or accident. It is designed to help maintain your lifestyle by ensuring your expenses can continue to be met during a period of absence from work, and is generally paid in instalments over an agreed period. If you have the responsibility of meeting regular mortgage repayments, this cover may save you from defaulting – the last thing you need at an already challenging time.

How do I decide which, if any, I need?

Your financial adviser or insurance broker will suggest you look at all of these options, but you may not necessarily choose to take them all up. At the end of the day, it's about paying a premium now to cover you in the event of possible outcomes. If, on reflection, you determine that you would manage in the future without needing insurance to help you get by, that could be the best outcome of all. Just make sure you've thought everything through. The premiums that you will pay for this type of policy are generally tax deductible.

Hot tip: If you hold your insurance within superannuation, your fund is able to claim a tax deduction on income protection insurance premiums, which can reduce the cost of the cover. However, be sure to closely review what you are – and aren't – covered for. You may want to look at some additional and/or separate coverage.

Do you need income protection?

While most of us insure our shiny material possessions, we rarely insure our income – arguably, the one thing you need most of all. Who else is going to fund your living expenses? Income insurance costs a very small percentage of your annual income for serious peace of mind. If you answer NO to any of the following, give this protection some good thought.

- Could you survive without your income? Who will pay the mortgage?
- Could you live comfortably on government support (Centrelink) benefits?
- Do you have enough sick leave to cover a long-term illness? (If you are self-employed, you don't have any sick leave!)
- If you ate into your savings to survive and weren't being paid superannuation, could you afford your retirement?

Do you need life, TPD or trauma insurance cover?
If you answer YES to any of the questions below, then you may need to consider life, TPD or trauma insurance cover:

● Do you have debts such as a mortgage, credit cards, personal loans? Or other loose ends which need resolving – HECS/HELP loan, or money owed to friends?
● Do you have dependants (children and/or ageing parents) with ongoing needs – medical and education expenses?
● Does your household rely partially or entirely on your income to maintain your mortgage repayments and existing lifestyle?

A solid structure

I know this chapter was a lot to take in; sorry-not-sorry. Although it can feel heavy going, it really is important to have considered and put these structures in place, so you are not burned later. And more importantly, to ensure that all the hard work you have done to secure your property is not wasted through poor or absent planning.

Okay, I promise we are DONE with the gloomy (albeit very necessary) serious talk. Next chapter we move onto the very, most funnest part . . . finding your perfect place.

● ● ● ● ● ●

CHARLOTTE, 30 – VIC

In 2017, I purchased an investment property in Bendigo with my brother and my parents. To be honest, it's a little bit of a mess! We are only now in the process of getting proper bank accounts and paperwork set up to show we are receiving equal amounts of rental income and contributing equal amounts to the mortgage.

The catalyst for finally doing this is that I'm now looking to purchase an apartment to live in. I have been told by a mortgage broker that the investment accounts need to be tidied up before they can help me!

My mum and dad's portion is in a trust account, which has made some of the bank admin annoying – bank statements can only be sent by post for them!

If I'd been more aware of stuff like this from the beginning, I would have discussed this with them. In an ideal world, I would sell the investment property to help me buy my own place, but the other parties are keen to hang on to it.

● ● ● ● ● ●

TAKE NOTE

There are many different types of properties, and two different ways to refer to them – the way in which they are generally referred to (including by government schemes) and their titles by law.

....

Property ownership types include options such as sole ownership, joint tenants and tenants in common. Choosing the right one for you will depend on both yours, and your co-owners' particular circumstances.

....

You know I'm a fan of a plan, and there's no more important plan than estate planning. Taking the time now will ensure your wishes are followed later.

....

While not having insurance can seem an easy way to reduce your spending, I urge you to think of it this way . . . any dollar you *never claim* on insurance is a dollar worth spending, because it means you've avoided all the pain and suffering that would have prompted the claim in the first place. Talking insurance could literally save your life – at least the one you dreamed of. And that, my friend, is worth everything.

....

Chapter 8

Finding the place that's right for you

When it comes to finding a place that suits you, what are you actually looking for? In the earlier chapters we began the research process – reviewing 'sold' listings, determining your budget, narrowing down your location and preferences. Now you're shored up with the important details, it's time to roll up your sleeves, mainline your lattes and keep hunting.

KEY TERMS

aspect: a fancy term for the direction a building faces, aspect determines the amount of light and warmth your property receives.

gross rental yield: a percentage figure calculated by dividing the annual income earned on a property by its sale price or market value.

off-the-plan property: a property where the building has not yet been constructed. This could be an apartment or town-house, or a house and land package.

strata report: a detailed report on the finances, insurance, building defects, planned maintenance, legal matters and meeting notes relating to a building's strata.

vacancy rates: how many rental properties are vacant in any particular area. Areas with a low vacancy rate are highly regarded by investors.

What kind of place are you looking for?

'Help, Victoria! There's so much information here and the sums are so high, I'm suffering from analysis paralysis. How do I decide what to buy?'

Take a deep breath, my friend! We've got this.

In Chapter 3, you laid out your property strategy. Working through a list of questions, you made a shortlist of the kinds of things you were looking for in your home and sorted this further by assigning each feature as either non-negotiable (must have), dealbreaker (walk away) or bonus (nice to have).

In light of your further work on budgets and lifestyle, is your dream property really your dream property for right now, or might it be a longer-term goal? Perhaps after reading through the last several chapters, you have revised your strategy . . . you might have decided to look at different types of purchases that could suit your short-to-medium term goal of getting into property, which might help you achieve your dream-home goal later down the line.

Armed with all the information you have gained, it's worth reviewing your plan one more time and writing a fresh list. All the decisions – from financing, to lifestyle considerations, to estate planning, structures and insurances – will affect your property hunt.

• •

REFINE YOUR PROPERTY WISHLIST

With all your research, now is a good time to review and refresh your key requirements from Chapter 3. Taking into consideration everything we've learnt so far, what are your five non-negotiables, five dealbreakers and five bonus features?

Non-negotiables

....

....

....

....

....

Dealbreakers

....

....

....

....

....

Bonus features

....

....

....

....

....

• •

To live in or to rent out?

Possibly the biggest question you're now asking yourself, is: am I buying this place to live in or buying it to rent out? And you might think that your answer will drastically affect what you're looking for in a home . . . not so fast.

No matter whether you are buying to live in or buying to rent out, the most important question you should ask yourself is: **is this a good investment?** Everything else – yes, including your non-negotiables and dealbreakers – is secondary.

Hot tip: Approach every property as if you're a valuer. It's so easy to fall in love with a place that's been styled by professionals – furniture brands offer pieces on consignment to property stylists as they know what great advertising it is – but you have to force yourself to look past the luxe lounges, rugs and paintings and take a good hard look at the block, building and neighbourhood with a critical eye.

Imagine you're Uncle Richard, determined to tell you what a bad buy you've made, along with a list of every possible thing wrong with the place. In the end, some of it won't matter to you, but you're much better off having looked that ugly duckling* directly in the eye and consciously decided whether to live with it or not, than ignoring it. *Not a literal duckling, obvs.

One final thing worth considering is that the improvements you can make to increase a property's value are somewhat limited when buying into a strata scheme. You have limited say on the common areas, and any renovations you may want to make to your own place must comply with the body corporate. There can be a lot of red tape and restrictions for anything more than a superficial change, such as painting an internal wall. External walls, even if they are on your title, will be managed by strata, and any substantial internal building works will need to be approved by them too. As always, it pays to read the fine print.

What to look for in a property

We've all heard the advice to 'buy the worst house on the best street' and no-one can miss the 'location, location, location' call-outs that regularly feature in property listings. And it's not just towns and suburbs you need to worry about. Even in a desirable suburb, there are more and less sought-after streets. Likewise, each block and building comes with a set aspect, which is equally important to consider.

The reason you see so many 'north-facing' lines spruiked in property listings is that, in Australia, this aspect is golden. (Literally.) Aspect affects how much light and warmth your property receives, and north-facing beauties win out. As much as we'd love it, we don't have the power to change the direction of the sun, so if you buy a place that faces south, it's guaranteed to be darker and colder than its north-facing neighbour. How much an aspect affects you will change during the course of the year, as the sun travels lower in the sky over a shorter period in winter. And beware a stunning sunset view – on long and late summer evenings, the heat and glare from that same aspect can be truly hideous.

The thing is: you *can* renovate, but you can't change the location or aspect of the property. Over time, it's normal to expect that, thanks to wear and tear and changing styles, the value of buildings on your property will decline. However, if you've bought well, the land will, ideally, appreciate. That's certainly what the bulk calculations on capital growth are based around. A particular risk is falling in love with a specific build or finish. If the location is poor, the chances of your property gaining in value are limited.

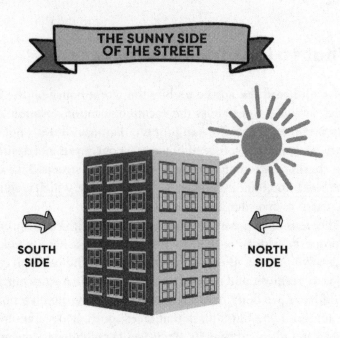

Location, location, location

Determining what makes a good location is different for everyone and is entirely dependent on your property strategy. The perfect location of your forever home may be vastly different from your ideal investment, or even your great-for-now first home, so it's important that you understand your goals. Is generating an immediate income the most important thing, or is it the potential capital growth, or is it to live in the bush far away from anyone and be self-sufficient? The strategies we'd develop for each of these is substantially different. Get clear on your goals before you start hunting around and save yourself time and heartache.

City or country? Depends! In either case, look for indicators of strong economic performance. In regional areas this could centre around a university or hospital or primary production – ideally, all with future development in the pipeline. Some regions are earmarked for development at a federal level. It's all about the long-term economic fundamentals of a place.

Accessibility. While it might be your dream to live far from the madding crowds, the vast majority of people need access to work. This may decline as technology (and pandemics) encourage remote working, but humans are social creatures, so the pull of central locations will likely remain strong. Holiday home locations seem ideal, but the further afield they are, the less strong their immediate capital growth is likely to be.

Common sense. Ask yourself: would you live here? Even if you never intend to, this question will help. If a place is poky, mouldy, with only one sink and sporadic running water, then it probably won't be appealing to anybody. While it's a good rule of thumb not to get emotionally attached to an investment purchase – that means letting the data do the talking, not ignoring basic standards of living – as a good landlord, you should always keep your tenants in mind.

Look around. Who's hanging in the hood? Is it families – young/old or elderly, empty nesters or young professionals? What's their lifestyle and what kind of housing do they want/need? Obviously what works for families (four beds, sprawling lawns, large garage) is very different to urban singles (studio apartment with high walkability) or an ageing population (no stairs, please!).

Local industry. How do people earn a living, locally? Are newly minted craft breweries shoring up the growth, or are long-term producers the mainstay? Is it a central urban hub or regional? Ideally, there'll be a variety of industries, key services (health, education) and manufacturing and distribution, as well as white-collar work, to sustain a broad population.

Finding the halo

It's easy to have a dream suburb or location – we all have one – but as we've discussed at length, the chances of that happening for us as first home buyers is reasonably slim.

Of course, different regions and areas have different prices. Even within states or cities and even suburbs, different locations will skew your property prices. Deciding where and what to buy, and your timing, are all important to consider. Historically, most places in Australia have increased in value over the long-term, but you might be wanting to see capital growth well before your 30-year mortgage is paid off, so a clear plan is important.

If you're buying to live and you're determined to live close to your dream suburb but can't afford it, then it could be as simple as expanding your location radius – something we're all too familiar with in recent years for other, unmentionable reasons. In the case of property hunting, this can be a super-savvy approach with extra benefits down the line. See, an established popular suburb or town will already have experienced its hockey-stick growth in housing prices, making it both less affordable to buy into and less likely to see further sharp rises.

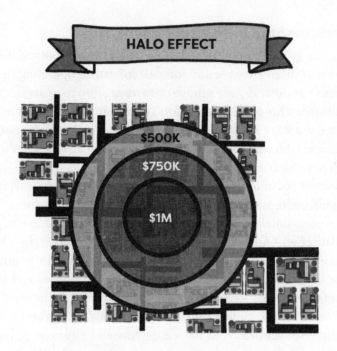

HALO EFFECT

$500K

$750K

$1M

Halo suburbs are more affordable

However, these high-performance locations tend to confer a 'halo effect' on surrounding areas, as buyers keen to live locally are happy to reside on the fringes at a price they can afford. Over time, with population growth, the neighbouring suburbs typically become absorbed into the values of the initial premium suburb. If you can get in before this happens, you will experience the uplift.

That's not to say this is guaranteed, for owner-occupiers or investors. Many an unlucky investor has been hooked into believing an area is on the brink of rapid growth only to have their investment languish in the doldrums for a decade. This is especially true of off-the-beaten-path towns earmarked for mining or other developments that never get off the ground or fail to grow in the ways predicted. So, expand your search by all means, but stay smart about it.

Investment in infrastructure

One way to determine if an area has high-growth potential is to review both the existing and forecast industries operating in and around the area. If your suburb or town is close to or serviced by healthcare (hospitals), education (universities) and supports at least a couple of major industries (say, agriculture and/or mining and/or established tourism), these are signs of a solid population with potential to grow.

Larger communities require infrastructure: roads, hospitals, schools, telecommunications. A good location prospect will have government funds committed to projects that are in the construction pipeline. Since the benefits of these services have yet to be realised, the major uplift in property values may not yet have happened, but once the services are operational and their benefits obvious, more residents will be attracted to the area.

That said, it's equally important to be aware of the flipside. Certain development can have a detrimental effect on property pricing. International airports are a good example. While such a large service may ultimately have a positive effect on local employment rates, it will also bring in noise and traffic, upsetting the lifestyle that had previously been enjoyed. During planning and construction and in the early years of operation, this could bring property values down. Over the longer term, its benefits may ultimately outweigh the downside and be an overall plus for your investment.

In either case, the area will never again be what it once was: a peaceful, rural enclave . . . If that was the dream you were buying into, say goodbye. I think the message is pretty clear on this one – it pays to be fully aware of any planned future developments in your area, both for good and bad down the line.

Check the insurance risk

Sadly, something increasingly important to be aware of is how insurable the property is. With natural disasters increasing in size, scale and frequency, insurers are becoming more careful in assessing a location's insurance risk. Just because a house has stood in a certain location for 100 years does not necessarily make it a safe bet today. Because of the changing weather conditions, many places close to rivers and flood plains are no longer considered reliably safe. The same goes for properties in bushy areas that are prone to fire.

One of the costs you must factor into your home ownership budget is ongoing upkeep and maintenance as well as damage repair, and sometimes, full replacement. If your place was destroyed by a disaster – man-made, natural or extraterrestrial (c'mon, they're out there) – could you afford to replace it without the help of insurance?

Even if you're a fully committed risk-averse insurance-loving diehard and have budgeted keenly for your premiums, it's worth checking with an insurer: can I even get this place insured in the first place? Based on a Climate Valuation report, the *Guardian* reported a list of Australian suburbs with a high proportion of 'high risk' properties, Port Melbourne, Brisbane City and Surfers Paradise among them.[49]

Already, post the 2022 floods, residents in towns like Forbes are finding their new insurance premiums prohibitively expensive. So, do your homework and never assume. The costs to insure may be more than you think, even if you're willing to pay for them.

Getting into the nitty-gritty

If you're keen to get into the nitty-gritty of property data (geeks, over here!), there is plenty you can review to get an idea of current and past property prices and the likely changes in values over time. This is particularly important for investors, but SOTM-savvy buyers of all types love to be in the know, right? If there's any way we can make extra money, either now or in the future, we like to hear about it. And renting out your home – whether short or long term, fully or partially – is one way to do it. Even if you have no practical plans for that, it's still worth factoring in a property's leasability, as this can be a good value indicator.

What you're looking for, essentially, in all these factors is whether the property is a good investment risk. If, for some reason, you had to offload it quickly, would it be easy to do, or might you be forced to sell at a loss? If you couldn't afford your mortgage, how leasable is the place – could you rent it out at a price that would cover your costs? Are there opportunities at hand, like the potential to improve the dwelling, or planned infrastructure developments?

You can pay for investment reports through various websites, but a lot of this data can be found online and through the property listings platforms. So, what are you looking at?

Median price. If you cast your mind back to Year 6 maths, you might remember that the median is the middle value in a set of data. When it comes to house prices, it is the sale price of the middle home in a list of properties ranked from highest sale price to lowest, over a set period of time. So if 100 houses were sold and ranked highest to lowest, the sale price of the fiftieth house would be the median house price.

Days on market. This measure shows the number of days a listing was on the market before it was sold. If the days on market number is low, it generally indicates there is high demand in the area and properties are selling quickly. If the days on market number is high, it generally indicates there is low demand and properties are on the market for a long period of time.

Vacancy rates. This is how many rental properties in the area are vacant. It is calculated as a percentage of dwellings in a rental property that is unoccupied at a particular time. Areas with a low vacancy rate will ensure a better yield for investors, as their properties are less likely to remain vacant after a tenant moves out.

Gross rental yield. A good way to compare the performance of different rental properties. Many people measure their returns using gross rental yield, which is a percentage figure calculated by dividing the annual income earned on the property by its sale price or market value.

Population and growth projections. Looking at the demographic data of an area will give you a good indication of the people who live there now and are likely to live there in future. Breakdowns by age, occupation and education give a guide to needs and interests, which can help fine-tune your strategy.

Building approvals. The Australian Bureau of Statistics collects monthly data relating to residential and non-residential building work above certain value limits that have been approved within the reference month and considers this an important leading economic indicator. The RLB Crane Index is used by industry as a simple indicator of the state of both the construction industry and country's economic health.[50]

Comparative recent sales

A key data set that a valuer looks at when deciding on a property's worth is what similar properties in the area have recently sold for. When comparing recent sales, the size of the block/lot, its aspect, accommodations (number of bedrooms, bathrooms and living space), and the condition of the property, are all factors. You can easily undertake a similar project for yourself by following the prompts outlined in Chapter 3, using the 'Sold' listing in property apps.

The longer you are on the property hunt, the more you can refine your results and insights. You can expand your search to 'For Sale' and begin a similar spreadsheet. Turning up to inspections in person will unearth details that are impossible to uncover remotely. Being able to see into the neighbour's bathroom, hear the noise of the flight path, smell hidden rising damp and bounce on loose floorboards can only be done in person. Add all these findings to your notes, and once the property sells, add it and its price to your 'Sold' table.

Over time you will build up an incredibly detailed knowledge of exactly which properties sold for the highest and lowest prices, and more importantly, why. This will arm you with the information you need to negotiate your best price and give you the confidence to jump in quickly when the right place shows up, as your research will have helped you determine what is, and what isn't, a good value purchase.

Buying an established property

Once you've narrowed down your location and list of features and you have a reasonable indication of budget from your 'Sold' spreadsheet, it's time to bust out your favourite sneakers and get amongst it. As outlined above, nothing beats turning up in person to check a place out. And it's kinda fun too (depending on how hungover you are). It can also be a brutal bloodbath out there, so let's line you up with a play-by-play to make this experience as enjoyable and productive as possible.

Saturdays are your days to get physical. If you're lucky enough to make a mid-week Wednesday inspection, good for you. The only real advantage to mid-week inspections is that they may give a little more breathing room and a quiet opportunity to speak one-on-one with the agent. However, you can equally make individual appointments if a place piques your interest, so don't worry if the first round is you + every other punter. In some ways this is good, as it gives you a better idea of the competitive interest in the property. Whenever you finally manage to get your (literal) foot in the door, the same process, as outlined below, applies.

1. **Do your research.** If you're scouring listings over your Saturday morning coffee, you are already too late. Do your research during the week while watching Netflix. Using one of the property listing apps, make a shortlist of properties you want to view, 'star' them and use the 'add to calender'

function to get their viewing times in your busy black book. Add as many as you want at this stage.

2. **Review and cull.** Friday night is the time to review your Saturday calendar. If you've been trigger-happy, you'll likely have several clashes. Check out each property you've shortlisted (again) and prioritise them in importance. Now, before you delete an inspection altogether, have a quick look at travel times. Maybe if you only spend ten minutes at one place and drive like Mario, you'll make it to the other apartment open at the same time. Or maybe you'll pull up out front of place number one on the day and decide that since the kebab shop next door makes it a flat-out no, you're gonna drive straight on. That's why I personally don't delete any listings from my calendar. Instead, I have some handy notes running alongside to make sure I get to my priority places as a must and any others are a bonus.

3. **Make friends with the agent.** When you arrive, the person who takes your name at the door is likely the main agent's assistant. While you won't be negotiating your deal with them, they often manage their boss's time, so be friendly and polite. (Be friendly and polite to everyone, really. The world has enough jerks!) During your inspections, make a point of introducing yourself to the agents and getting to know them. Even if this isn't the right place for you, discuss with them what is. Let them know your timeframe for buying and what you're looking for. If you're super keen, cashed-up and ready to buy the first place that's suitable, let them know that too. In either case, keep in contact. This is the best way (apart from using a buyer's agent) to get offered off-market viewings (a preview of a place that the agent's just signed before it officially hits the market).

4. **Look around. Carefully.** Put your valuer goggles on and look straight past the styling and imported furnishings. Imagine the place empty. Does it suit your essential criteria or offer

something new? Are there things that don't quite suit, but which you could make work, or are there dealbreakers? Here is a list of things to look out for:

a. **Walls** – look for any stains or cracks, peeling paint or bubbles in the ceilings and walls. They could indicate a leaky pipe or water ingress (coming in from outside). *Hot tip:* Look out for freshly painted walls. While it might have been done just to freshen up, it could also be to hide damage. Be wary.

b. **Floors** – bowing, sagging or creaking floorboards, or gaps in the floorboards, lifting edges on the lino, chipped tiles, unevenly spongy, springy, wet and/ or stained carpets. These may indicate the whole house needs restumping, or simply, an indication of a gracefully ageing beauty. Either way, best to get them professionally reviewed.

c. **Doors and windows** – open and shut every single one. Completely. Do they close smoothly or get stuck? If the latter, look more closely – is the timber swollen at the edges? Is there a gap between the door/window and its frame (top, bottom, sides)? Creaking much? These could all indicate water leaks and poor insulation, not to mention being a security hazard.

d. **Cupboards** – check how these operate and the storage inside. A good clue as to how well the vendor (if the place isn't tenanted) looks after the place, is how tidy they keep their cupboards. Yes, this can feel pervy. No, it's not bad to do.

e. **Feel around** – poke your head into wardrobes and understair cupboards and run your fingers across their ceilings, floors and sides. Is there any mould, mildew or residual damp?

f. **Use your nose** – you might not be able to see or feel it, but your nose can be a pretty reliable indicator of something funky going on behind the walls or beneath the floor. Don't ignore bad or off smells; have your building and pest inspector look into them more thoroughly.

g. **Bathrooms and laundry** – if ever you're going to have water problems, it will be in, around and under tiling. You'd be shocked at the extent of poor or damaged waterproofing out there – it's enough to get mushrooms growing up and through your grout (believe me, I've been there). While mould and mildew may indicate problems, you'll really need professional meters to test for problems here.

h. **Storage** – what storage is there in the kitchen, bedrooms, study, garage, garden shed, etc. Is there enough for you and your enviable collection of (insert favourite vice here)?

i. **Gardens/outdoor** – how well maintained are the gardens and outdoor spaces? Once again, a well-kept garden can be the sign of a well-kept home.

j. **Exterior walls and footings** – look for flaking, bubbling or lifting paint where the wall meets the ground, this can indicate rising damp. Ensure that there is clearance between the foundations and garden beds which are a breeding ground for hungry wood-eating pests like termites.

k. **Stand outside** – for a while and have a good listen. Is it noisy? What's the traffic like? Get nosy – who are your neighbours? Is there a school or day care or other social centre that might create a lot of noise at certain times of the day? How about industrial machinery, cars, motorbikes or other loud engines?

l. **Take in the view** – get a good idea of the direction in which the place faces and how much light and warmth it receives. If possible, come back (or at least drive past) at a few different times of the day, so you can get a well-rounded idea of the changing conditions.

m. **Ask to operate** – if the place has a gas heater or air-conditioning or any other mod-cons installed, ask to get them turned on and operating. If the agent says no and you're keen to move forward, insist on testing these during your pest and building inspection.

5. **Speak to the neighbours.** The best people to speak to about the property you're looking at purchasing are the neighbours. Is there any loud construction nearby, or any other factors that could impact your enjoyment of the property? Is the strata scheme poorly run? It pays, literally, to ask. Don't worry about feeling awkward – just go for it!

6. **Pick up a brochure and contract.** Whether you're keen or not, it's useful to collect brochures and contracts, especially in the early days of hunting. It's worthwhile getting familiar with property contracts and learning how to read them.

7. **Respond to the follow-up call.** Again, whether you're intending to buy now or in three years' time, it's important to cultivate good relationships with the agents. They'll follow up with you on Monday or Tuesday, asking where your interests lie. Be polite and respond.

8. **Schedule next steps.** If you're keen to proceed, you'll ask the agent to email a contract, which you should forward to your lawyer. Book in a pest and building inspection at the same time.

• •

YOUR INSPECTION CHECKLIST

Using the prompts above, create your own 'inspection checklist' that you can bring with you on your property hunts to ensure you give each place a good going over.

☐ ....

☐ ....

☐ ....

☐ ....

☐ ....

☐ ....

● ●

Building and pest inspection

If you're keen on the place, it's important to run a pest and building inspection. Often, as detailed in Chapter 4, these can be combined. These days, many vendors will offer access to the inspection they ran. The agent may also direct you to a central service which you pay a nominal fee to access, and the balance, if you are the successful bidder. While both of these can be cost-effective options, you have to ask yourself if you're getting an agenda-free report.

If you can, it's probably worth engaging your own specialist. The advantage here is that, since you are the client, you can walk through the place with your inspector. It's not necessary, but I would try to make time to do that if I could. That way you can point out all the potential issues you noticed during your own viewing and ask them to assess how critical they are and what they might potentially cost to fix. Since some details they will only share off the record (due to professional indemnity), you may get a lot more helpful information and better insight this way.

According to the NSW Fair Trading, an inspector will look at the following areas to check for any problems: interior, exterior, roof space, under floor space, roof exterior, site of the property.

In reality, some are lazier than others and will use the excuse of 'furniture being in the way' as a reason to not fully complete checking certain areas. That's why it often pays to develop a relationship with a builder you trust.

Hot tip: See if you can pay them a little extra for a fully detailed review, which might include advice on any immediate rectification or renovation building works you are planning in the immediate future. This can be invaluable when it comes to determining your budget.

Strata report

If you're buying into a strata scheme, your building inspection will generally only cover the lot's interior and immediately outside the unit. The real estate agent must give you a copy of any by-laws in place, which includes rules for the building, such as pets and guidelines for common areas.

If you want to have the common property areas inspected, you'll need to request a special-purpose report. You can pay a professional company to analyse and compile the key information. You can also inspect the strata records yourself via the strata manager. For this, you will need the seller's permission and to pay a fee to the owner's corporation.

Reviewing a strata report will give you a comprehensive look at everything you need to know, including a scope of the finances, insurance, building defects, any planned maintenance, legal matters and meeting notes. Read the meeting notes carefully – they could tell you a lot about any planned essential work, which could have an impact on the levies you pay.

Watch-outs for buying off the plan

Buying off the plan or buying land that's not registered comes with its own unique challenges. For a start, there's nothing to inspect – at least in terms of a building. However, you can still (and should) run your valuation research to determine its prospects as a worthwhile investment.

'Victoria, what do you mean by "buying off the plan"?'

Properties can be advertised for sale before the building has been constructed. Buying this type of property is known as 'buying off the plan'. This phrase is typically applies to apartments (lots) being built in large multi-residential developments. For those wanting a family home, another common offer, particularly targeted at first home buyers or investors, are house and land packages. This is a similar thing, just a different type of dwelling and ownership scheme.

When you buy off the plan, you're committing to paying a price for a property that is, as yet, an unknown quantity. What you're sold and what you end up paying for may end up completely different, with the end product not only differing from your expectations, but also perhaps worth less by the time it is finished.

If it gets finished. Over the last couple of years, a significant number of builders and developers have gone out of business in Australia, so incompletion is a real issue. Without being an alarmist (since there are several protections in place to limit this), if a company goes bust, there is the potential they could take your money and leave you with nothing to show for it.

In addition, there is also the issue of poor building quality and defects, as we've seen several times in the news. It's important to read the contract, as typically there will be allowances for the builder to compromise on the floorplan and finishes, which may mean you end up with a product that's far from what you originally had in mind. So, while often these packages may seem more affordable than a finished product with similar attributes, there are real risks involved.

READING THE FINE PRINT

Do your due diligence

Buyer beware

Whether buying an existing or future dwelling, all will come with a sales contract. Before you get serious about putting in an offer, you'll want to have the contract reviewed by a legal professional who specialises in property. Their job is to advise you of any potential risk, so some of their recommendations may initially seem to be over the top. Remember, they're lawyers and their job is to protect their client (you!). If your lawyer starts agitating around terms on the contract that you don't understand or agree with, ask! You're the client and you're paying for the service. It is your right to ask as many questions as you want and your responsibility to understand exactly what the heck you're getting yourself into.

Anything you don't understand or agree with is worth discussing with them. Since their ultimate purpose is to help you achieve your goal while avoiding problems, if you clearly explain your objectives, they may think of other solutions and can adjust their approach to serve you better.

Once they have your brief, they will engage with the vendor's solicitor, negotiating where necessary, under your instruction, to arrive at a contract with terms agreeable to you, which we'll go through in detail in the next chapter.

At the end of the day, it is up to you to do your due diligence on every front and ensure that the property you are committing to meets all your needs. It's fine if you're prepared to buy a fixer-upper, so long as you know that's what you're signing up for. So get those inspections done and negotiate anything that needs to be amended, before you sign on the dotted line.

● ● ● ● ● ●

EMMA, 26 – NSW

Originally, in 2021, we signed with a broker and had pre-approval completed with my partner's parents going guarantor. In March 2022, we signed a contract for an off-the-plan apartment, but nine months after signing the contract, due to the increased cost of building materials, the apartments had not yet commenced building.

Our deposit was returned and we started looking at properties. After finding a house we wanted to purchase, our solicitor provided us with contacts to have a building and pest inspection completed. We are forever grateful we spent the extra money to have this completed as the house had live termites, rotting wood, high moisture, black mould and the list goes on. Luckily we had not put any deposit down, so only had the cost of the building and pest inspection.

We then found another house we were interested in. We commenced the same process and had the building and pest completed, although the real estate had already done their own. Thankfully again, we had paid the money to have our own building and pest completed. The report came back recommending that a builder provide a further quote for the roof. We didn't think it would be much of an issue, so we paid our deposit to hold the property while we had the roof inspected. On the final day of our cooling-off period, the builder provided us with a quote for the roof of $30,000, advising that urgent repairs were required to make it habitable.

Our solicitor provided this quote and a request for the property price to be reduced, which was declined. We decided not to proceed with the purchase and lost 0.25 per cent of our deposit.

After a two-month break from looking, we decided to start the hunt again in the early months of 2023. We found a house that cleared our building and pest inspection. To purchase the house, we utilised the first home buyer scheme and super saver, without which we would not have been able to reach the total needed.

While this was not the journey we thought we would have, we learned a lot along the way and are now happily in a place that's standing and we can proudly call our own!

● ● ● ● ● ●

TAKE NOTE

Whether you buy off the plan or an established home, it's important you do your homework. Do your online research then hit the pavement and get to inspections. Nothing beats gathering in-person data with all your senses.

....

Being clear on your own goals and objectives is important, as no doubt you will need to compromise on some of your wants if getting into property is a real SOTM (specific, optimistic, time-based, measurable) goal of yours.

....

Ask yourself, and answer truthfully, the most important question: **is this property a good investment?**

....

Chapter 9

Purchasing, from go to woah

Once you have found your property and your due diligence is underway, things can very serious (and very exciting!) very quickly. This chapter will talk you through the process of buying a property, from negotiation to settlement. With all the work and time you've put in getting to this stage, this period can feel like a bit of a whirlwind – it will go by super fast and before you know it, you'll have the keys to your new home in your hands!

KEY TERMS

auction: a public way of selling a property that happens at a set time and place, with no cooling-off period.

buying off market: purchasing a property that has not been publicly listed for sale.

bridging loan: a short-term loan taken out to cover the time between settling on a property purchase and finalising a long-term property loan, typically offered at a much higher interest rate.

exchange: when the vendor accepts the buyer's offer. Each signs a contract and they swap them. At this time, the buyer also hands over their deposit.

private treaty: when a property is offered for sale under no set timeframe, with offers privately negotiated and given a cooling-off period.

settlement: the date for completion of the contract.

Finding a place

In previous chapters, we've covered in detail how to find, shortlist and assess properties through the regular channels of advertised listings – namely, the property-finder apps. It's important you do this research to get a good feel of the market and what you're willing to spend.

But the way that the competition is these days, it can also be completely disheartening, with too few places and too many buyers, all of whom seem to have way more cash than you. What's a smart-but-cash-poor millennial to do?

'Help, Victoria! Are there other ways to find a place?'

The short answer, my love, is YES! In fact, that's exactly how I found mine. By going through a buyer's advocate, we found a place off market. The owner was keen to sell and the property had some obvious issues, so we were able to negotiate a great price. However, the opportunity came with a 24-hour time limit. Thankfully, because our finance was pre-approved and I had a builder I could call in last-minute to give me a comprehensive report, including rough cost estimates on the things that needed fixing, we could make it happen. As always, it pays to be organised!

You can also buy property off the plan, which of course isn't listed in the same way as an established property is.

How to buy off the plan

In the previous chapter we discussed the pros and cons of buying off the plan. But if this was something you were interested in, how would you go about it?

For the most part, these types of opportunities are made available through developers, who buy the land as a large parcel and then subdivide and/or submit development plans to create smaller lots which they sell off, either as: units/apartments in a multi-residential construction which they build; as house-and-land packages, which they project manage on your behalf; or as land allotments that you can self-build on.

Though sometimes these may be advertised on the property apps, generally, the developer will set up various channels for you to enquire and evaluate through. Depending on the size of the development, they can include a website, a sales office, or even whole display homes and villages. In some ways, this is similar to building through a home-building development company, and the developer will usually be related to or working with such groups when there is single-dwelling construction involved.

How to buy off market

We don't want to just consider the properties that have been publicly listed. Oh no, we're smarter than that! Because at any moment, there are literally thousands of properties around Australia with the potential to be bought. If you manage to buy this way, it's called buying off market. So, how do you find or create the opportunity to access them?

If they aren't listed on real estate websites or the property apps and don't have a giant FOR SALE sign out the front, then how on earth do you find them? While it's a little harder than the usual route, there are lots of ways you can find an off-market gem; you just need to know where to look.

Real estate agents

As I've said many times in the book, even though they advocate for the seller, it's well worth getting cosy with your local real estate agents. At the end of the day, they're most interested in selling houses. If you let them know that you're cashed up and ready to buy, they will actively keep an eye out for you, effectively becoming a buyer's advocate. Since, in these cases, you're looking to buy 'off list', the agent is as much on the hunt for a new opportunity as any buyer's agent out there.

Buyer's agents

Using a buyer's agent is like supersizing the previous strategy. Since buying houses for others is their full focus, buyer's agents make it their purpose to be well connected and across the market. They are not limited to the stock and contacts of one particular real estate agent, but have access to many. Buyer's agents make it their job to be up-to-date with trends and have research tools at their fingertips, and because they're constantly bringing new buyers to the table, they are often the first person a real estate agent will call if their client has asked them to quietly test the market. Because it's their skillset and they know the real estate agent well, they can often negotiate a better deal for their buyer.

Buyer's agents are perfect for people who are time poor and who know what they want, but don't have the time to attend multiple inspections and to do all of the grunt work and are willing to pay someone else to do so. They charge roughly 2 per cent of the purchase price, as their job is a little more hands on than a real estate agent (you'll often find buyer's advocates knocking on the doors of people who aren't even selling).

Do it yourself

Of course, in terms of finding and creating off-market opportunities, agents use a variety of tactics that you can also follow yourself – for free!

Off-market websites. Some sellers prefer to quietly list a place without having to pay agent's fees. Often they're not in a hurry to sell, but will do so for the right price. DIY sellers will list on websites such as Listing Loop or Property Whispers or, depending on the location, in local classifieds.

Word of mouth. Ask around to see if anyone you know is aware of someone looking to sell who might be tempted by the idea of not paying advertising and agent's fees. It's amazing how many friends of friends in the neighbourhood, especially as kids move out of home, are thinking of downsizing or relocating. Your prompt may be just the push they never knew they needed.

Community social groups. Similarly, join the local community Facebook groups and keep an eye on anyone looking to sell.

Letterbox drop. Pop a note into the letterbox of your dream house asking if they'd consider selling. I know more people than you would believe who've managed to buy property this way.

Benefits of buying off market

- Less competition – there are no other buyers in the mix.
- Convenient and efficient – it saves time in inspecting places that don't suit your wants or needs.
- More flexibility – both parties are often more willing to negotiate.

How to buy property in Australia

'Victoria, how exactly do you go about buying property in Australia?'

There are two primary ways to buy property in Australia: private treaty or auction.

Private treaty, in its broadest practice, is when a property is offered for sale under no set timeframe, with offers privately negotiated and given a cooling-off period.

Auctions, on the other hand, happen at a set time and place in a public forum and, if the bidder is successful, i.e. the vendor accepts the bid, there is no opportunity to back out.

Let's look in detail at how the process works for each.

Private treaty

Buying through private treaty is when a property is listed on the market and its sale terms (price and contract) are negotiated *in private* with the seller or real estate agent. While this can take the stress of high-pressure bidding out of the process, it can bring its own challenges.

Being private, this process is not always transparent. As a buyer, you don't know how many other people are placing offers for a home, or even what prices they're talking. Frankly, whatever the agent is telling you could be a whole lotta codswallop, though that would be completely unethical. On the seller's side, there is no fixed deadline on the sale, which may reduce the heat of competition. As such, there are several strategies that agents and you – the buyer – can use to replicate an auction-like environ-ment, some which are often used to joint advantage and others which are very much frowned upon.

Standard process

As a buyer, there's a general process to follow if you'd like to buy a home this way:

1. Ask the seller for the contract of sale as soon as possible and have it reviewed by a licensed conveyancer or solicitor.
2. Organise (or have your conveyancer organise) building, pest and/or strata reports.
3. Get conditional finance or pre-approval.
4. Make an offer for the home verbally, such as over the phone, or in writing, like an email.
5. Negotiate the sale price of the home with the real estate agent or seller.

Sometimes, real estate agents are eager to finalise the sale of a home, but remember, they can't use high-pressure tactics or harassment to persuade you to make an offer.

Once negotiations are complete and your offer has been accepted by the seller, the next step is to exchange the contract of sale. Until contracts are exchanged, the sale of the home isn't finalised, which means the buyer or seller can pull out of the sale, or the seller may negotiate with other buyers for a higher offer.

Gazumping

Gazumping occurs when your offer has been verbally accepted, but then, before contracts are exchanged, the vendor accepts another offer – usually for a higher amount. While Australian law advises that agents are duty bound to inform both serious buyers and the vendor of any and all bona-fide offers up until exchange of contracts, there are ways around this. For example, the vendor can instruct an agent not to advise of offers under a certain price, or a vendor can delay exchange.

It can be extremely disappointing, not to mention costly, if this happens, as neither the agent nor seller is obliged to compensate you for any money you may have spent on legal advice, inspection reports, finance application costs or inquiries if you are gazumped, though any expression-of-interest payment must be refunded to you in full.

Waiving cooling-off certificate

Though, typically, the conditions of a private treaty process include a cooling-off period for buyers, in most states in Australia, buyers can attach an addendum to their signed contract to waive this. You will need your lawyer's help to do so – it has a different name in each state.

Attaching this waiver shows a buyer's commitment and often hastens the offer-acceptance-and-exchange process, reducing the opportunity for competitors to negotiate against you.

Expressions of Interest (EOI)

To create an artificial auction-type deadline, agents will sometimes list a property as 'For sale by expressions of interest (EOI)'. This generally requires interested parties to submit their best offer by the due date. The vendor will consider all offers on the table at that point and decide which, if any, they will accept. This is quite the game of chess, as if you lowball, you may not be invited to participate in the post-deadline negotiations (and don't fool yourself – even if the agent says there won't be any, if there are two offers on the table that are super close, of course further offers will be invited). But if you go too high, you may end up paying a lot more than you'd have preferred.

Auction

Auctions can be a great way to score a property quickly and at a good price, depending on the market. But there are some important things to know before heading to an auction with your heart in your hand – which, by the way, is never a good idea. Auctions require your best poker face. They are competitive, sometimes cutthroat and often occur in front of a big crowd, with the winner taking all. (Cue dramatic music!)

A property auction is typically conducted by a licensed auctioneer and can be held onsite (at the property), or at a venue, like a real estate office. At the end of the auction, the property is sold to the highest bidder and the sale is unconditional (meaning there's no cooling-off period). Everything plays out in public at an auction – what you see is what you get.

Be prepared

Auction campaigns run quickly – usually over a four-week period – so if you're intending to buy this way, you need to be well prepared in advance. Many of the same guidelines for negotiating a private treaty sale apply here, you're just doing it under extreme time constraints, so review that list again and get yourself organised and on the front foot.

Have your loan pre-approved and know the market. As with any property, attend several open inspections and arrange private ones at different times of the day if you can. If you are serious about bidding, complete your building and pest inspections, and based on all your research, set yourself a 'walkaway' price.

Have your lawyer review and adjust the contract before auction day. If you are the successful bidder, you are obliged to proceed under the terms in the contract that's been agreed, so make sure it's one you're onboard with.

Pre-auction offers

It's common for agents to set an auction campaign with the primary intention of creating artificial time constraints and increasing competition among buyers. Very often, both they and the vendor may be willing to accept offers prior, and will happily exchange before the auction date.

It is worth asking the agent if they are willing to accept offers prior to auction, and show your interest early, to ensure you don't miss out.

Practise

Watching other auctions is a good way to ease yourself into the process and get a sense of what the competition is like. If you can't get to one in person, many property auctions are also livestreamed through sites like Gavl or Anywhere Auctions.

It can be fun registering and practising bidding at smaller auctions with less at stake. Many large auction houses sell off the contents of private estates, or run speciality art and jewellery auctions both online and in person. You can pick up mismatched fine-bone china for less than $10, so it's a low-risk, high-reward way to test run your bidding skills.

On the day

Wake up fresh! If the property goes to auction, it's a tense day for all. Make sure you get a good night's sleep and follow your normal morning routine. The last thing you want to do is turn up hungover or jittery. You need your wits about you! After all, you may just be making the biggest purchase of your life.

Decide beforehand who is bidding. If you don't feel confident, nominate someone you trust to bid for you. This is where a buyer's agent can be helpful, or a trusted friend, family member or colleague. Most importantly, make sure they're aware of your walkaway price. It's also worth running through various strategies with them and ensuring you're comfortable with the proposed tactics. Be clear on any you don't want them to pursue.

Have your finance in order. If you are the winning bidder, you will be obliged to exchange contracts and transfer the agreed deposit on the spot. You will need to have enough funds for this on the day, and be confident that your loan will be in place come settlement day.

Set a ceiling price. Ensure you have funds at the ready to cover the deposit – a percentage, as stated in the contract, of the final price. While you have no idea what the winning bid will be, you do have control over how much you can afford and are willing to spend yourself. Set your upper limit and don't go beyond it.

Register. While this isn't a legal requirement in Australia, most agencies like to set up a registration system to get an idea of how many buyers might be attending an auction. To register, you'll need to provide your name, address and contact information to the auctioneer, along with some ID.

Tactics

When it comes to the actual day, it's good to have a bidding strategy in mind. This includes having preset your bidding ceiling and strategies, such as whether bidding in odd or even, big or small increments.

Tactics such as this can be a good way to outmanoeuvre other bidders. Bold increments can show that your intentions are clear, while small incremental bids can also work to your advantage, as they disrupt the bidding pattern and throw off the other buyers.

Another tactic is waiting until the last minute to place a bid. If you've ever attended an auction, you might notice someone raise their paddle for the first time just as the auctioneer is calling last bids. This approach lets you gauge the competition and can eliminate intense bidding wars, but it can also be risky. You miss the opportunity to assert yourself as a strong buyer early on.

A strong early bid asserts your dominance and can scare off other bidders. On the other hand, if you start low, it can create a flurry of early interest which will blow out excited punters who tire later.

Auctions are very much a game of chess, which is why they can be so nerve-racking – or fun, if that's your schtick.

Regardless of which strategy you go with, remember: keep your emotions in check, stick to your game plan and stay focused. Be alert and ready to act fast, as auctions can move extremely quickly – in some cases, they're over in a matter of minutes.

Auction rules

There are several terms and rules to auctions, which are important to understand.

The reserve. This is the minimum price the vendor is willing to accept for the property. If the reserve isn't reached, the vendor may choose not to sell on the day. As soon as an auctioneer announces that the property is 'on the market', that means that the vendor will accept the highest bid from then on.

Passed in. Until the auctioneer calls 'on the market', any bids made on the day, even if they are within the price guide, won't necessarily be enough to make the sale, and, ultimately, the auctioneer may 'pass in' the property. This means it hasn't sold at auction.

First right to negotiate. If you're keen on the place, it's still worth making a bid, even if the auction goes flat. If a property passes in, the highest bidder has first rights to post-auction negotiations – where you privately negotiate with the auctioneer and vendor (assuming the vendor is willing), to see whether both parties can reach agreement.

Vendor's bid. Sometimes if it's a quiet auction and no-one is bidding, the auctioneer will place a 'vendor's bid' on behalf of the seller, to get the ball rolling. If the property passes in on a vendor's bid, no-one gets first rights to negotiate.

Negotiating

Whichever way you have found a place, and whichever purchasing path you follow, you will eventually come to this point: negotiating.

How you buy – private treaty or auction – will affect your negotiations. There is also more room to negotiate on an established property than off the plan; however, in every instance, you must ensure that the sales contract is suitable to you. You can request changes.

When negotiating, it helps to keep the following in mind.

Be aware of the market. Review comparable property prices, ideally as close in time as possible to your purchase. Australian property markets, especially in major cities, move quickly.

Consider an independent valuation. This could be an option, especially if you request that it includes a consultation if you're planning future improvements/renovations. However, it's also worth bearing in mind that valuer's positions do vary.

Set your walkaway price. Before you start negotiating, have a set figure in mind based on your research and budget. This will help take the emotion out of it.

Get to know the seller's motivations. This is where getting friendly with the agent helps – they can give you the inside intel. If you know that they're keen to sell due to divorce or are downsizing and not in a rush, this could help fine-tune your strategy.

Get friendly with the sales agent. While their priority is to serve their client, securing a committed buyer will help them achieve that.

Use your research. Use any defects or issues that come up in your research – either from the building and pest report, or infrastructure planning in the neighbourhood – to negotiate a better price.

Be finance ready. Have your loan pre-approved and check in with your lender/broker regarding this particular property so you can move quickly and with confidence.

Remain calm, clear and professional. While you can (and should) use proven negotiating tactics, such as setting time and price limits, don't engage in any threatening or mean behaviour.

Work with an expert property lawyer. They will alert you to any conditions in the contract and assist with changes or additions – such as special conditions or waivers – which could help you move more quickly with peace of mind.

● ●

NAME YOUR WALKAWAY PRICE

Before you turn up to bid at auction, it's important to have already set your walkaway price. This will help ensure you don't get caught up in the emotion of the day. Write your walkaway price here (don't forget to have included in your budget, the extra 'hidden costs' we discussed in Chapter 6).

....

● ●

Negotiating the terms

There are two key things you'll negotiate when it comes to buying a property: the terms of the contract and the price.

Before we go any further, I want to be very clear that you can negotiate the conditions of a contract of sale in both private treaty and auction. The only difference is that, under auction conditions, this must be done well in advance of bidding, as there is no cooling-off period (time to change your mind about the sale).

Before agreeing to the contract, take a careful look through – and have your lawyer take an even *more* careful look through – to see if there are any terms you'd like to negotiate. Your solicitor will help you with this, and it's worth preparing for the possibility of a bit of back and forth between you and the seller before reaching an agreement.

Remember, it's important to carefully review your contract and understand any terms and conditions of the sale before signing, which your lawyer will be able to explain to you. Here are a few common sales conditions you might negotiate in your contract.

Deposit. The deposit amount will be specified, usually as a percentage, as well as holding and release terms.

Settlement date. The settlement date is when the final payment is made and your conveyancer will complete the relevant forms to have the property transferred from the seller's name to yours.

Subject to finance. If you're relying on financing, such as a loan from a bank, you could push for your contract to include a 'subject to finance' clause, which allows you to back out of the sale if your financing doesn't come through by the settlement date.

Subject to building inspection. Similarly, this clause allows you to pull out of the sale if anything major is revealed in the building inspection, like significant damage or defects, that may change your mind about the purchase.

Chattels and fixtures. No, these aren't props from a Western. Chattels are appliances, finishes and fittings which theoretically could be moved (such as a dishwasher, curtains or light fittings), but which have often been purpose fit so would be difficult to replace. Anything that is fixed, such as built-in joinery, is automatically included – but if you're not sure, ask.

Cooling-off period. A cooling-off period depends on which state you live in, but if it is a legal requirement in your state, this should be outlined in the contract. Remember, a cooling-off period is a timeframe where you can back out of the sale a few days after making an offer with a minor penalty.

Hot tip: Don't haggle over the small stuff. If the vendor wants to take their prize roses from the front garden, then unless it's the main reason you're buying the place, let them have them. Be sure to address anything that may be costly for you to rectify or adjust later, but things like curtains are replaceable.

Negotiating the price

As a SOTM research star, you'll have put a lot of effort into determining the relative pricing of places similar to yours. You'll have a good idea of your budget, have your finance pre-approved and be ready to make an offer as soon as you find the right property. So let's make sure you get it.

If you are buying privately, here are my top negotiation tips.

Submit your offer. To be in with a chance, you need to submit a serious offer. You can do this in one of three ways:

1. Verbal offer – tell the agent what you're willing to pay.
2. Written offer – submit an offer in writing via email.
3. Contract of sale – sign a contract of sale and fill out details of your offer.

This is what gets the ball rolling and is usually not the one and only offer you'll make. The agent will take your offer to the vendor and they will discuss it. A good agent will be trying to balance getting their client the best price possible with ensuring they finalise the sale. If the vendor is too greedy, they may end up with no buyers. If they roll over at the first offer, they may get less than what the market was willing to pay. As such, the agent will likely come back and forth on price and terms a few times – with you and every other interested buyer.

Stay involved. If you've shown that you're an active and able buyer, the agent should keep you informed of any other offers on the table. This can sometimes feel as if they are playing you off against the other buyers, but mostly, they are just trying to get the best result for their client and giving you the best opportunity to participate. Whether you stay in the negotiations or not is ultimately up to you.

Be confident. Everyone has a first time going through something like this and it's ALWAYS nerve racking. Put your best game face on and enjoy the process as best you can.

Know when to fold 'em. Know your limits and know when to walk away. There will always, always, ALWAYS be another property, even if it doesn't feel like it at the time. It is NEVER worth compromising your budget so much that you end up destroying the life you've worked so hard to create.

Exchanging contracts

Once you've had your offer accepted, and finalised any other terms in the contract, you and the seller are ready to exchange contracts. At that point you'll enter into a legally binding contract for the purchase of the property.

Deposit

You will usually be required to pay a deposit at the time of exchange, and the exchange won't be formalised until this is received. The deposit terms are written into the contract and while the cost varies, it is usually around 10 per cent of the sale. (This is different from the deposit your lender requires of you; it's a deposit to secure the property.) This security deposit is usually held in the real estate agent's trust account and cannot be released without the agreement of both seller and vendor, which is part of the settlement process.

Exchange

You will sign a copy of the contract, as will the vendor. Your lawyers will exchange these so you each end up with (or at least, your lawyer will) the copy signed by the other party. You are now legally bound to complete the sale by the terms of the contract. This will include settlement date.

Settlement

The date for completion, or settlement, is written into the contract. This happens at a time agreed by all parties, somewhere between 9 am and 4 pm, typically around mid-to-late afternoon. The exact time will depend on several factors, including how proactive your solicitors are and how quickly the banking system processes the transactions.

'Victoria, I want to get in ASAP! What affects completion time?'

A lot of other people (and things) must do their jobs in a proactive and timely manner to make sure you can collect the keys at a reasonable time on completion day. In Australia, settlement is most commonly facilitated securely and electronically through online platform PEXA, which means settlement can occur seamlessly within a few hours. However, you're still relying on:

The lender. To make funds available.

The solicitor. To ensure that funds are disbursed according to their client's instructions.

The real estate agents. To facilitate the process.

The seller. To vacate and hand over the keys.

If things aren't happening within expected timeframes, pick up the phone and chase your lender/broker, lawyer and/or real estate agent. This is not a time to sit back and be polite.

Vacant possession

In most states, the seller needs to provide vacant possession by settlement, which means they need to have removed all their items and vacated the property by then. For example, if settlement is scheduled to complete at 2.30 pm, then the seller will need to have left by then and handed the keys to the agent. It is good practice to have vacated no later than the morning of settlement day to avoid any dispute from the buyer about you being ready to settle.

If there are tenants in the property, but the buyers are buying the property with vacant possession, then the same rule applies to them. The exception is in Western Australia. In this case, the standard form of contract provides that you generally do not need to move out until midday on the day following settlement.

If something goes wrong

It would be nice if every property negotiation and purchase went off without a hitch, but things can, and do, go wrong. It's worth knowing what your options are if, for whatever reason, you change your mind.

Cooling-off period. Unless you buy at auction, a standard property contract comes with a cooling-off period for the buyer. Depending on the state/territory, it's somewhere between two and five business days after exchanging contracts, except in Western Australia and Tasmania, which have no cooling-off periods.

The seller cannot rescind once contracts have been exchanged, but the buyer can invoke their right to withdraw according to the contract terms. However, in some states, you'll have to pay a forfeiture fee – anywhere from .25 per cent, up to the full amount of the deposit, plus any penalties.[51] So, not cheap, but certainly a lot less than a massive mortgage for a property you don't feel good about.

Buying at auction. If you pull out after winning at auction, you will be in breach of contract (at auction, once the gavel falls, the highest bidder is in a legally binding contract with the seller). The penalty for withdrawing could be the full deposit.

Pre-settlement inspection. The vendor is responsible for keeping the property in good condition until settlement, and the buyer has the right to a pre-settlement inspection before the property finalises. If the buyer unearths any issues – such as a new water leak that's damaged floorboards – any amendments to the contract (price, etc.) must be negotiated before settlement. It is very unlikely you will be able to back out of the sale altogether, so both sides will work to reach a fair agreement. Once you have settled, there is little chance of claiming any damages, so it's important to conduct that final inspection carefully.

Issues delaying settlement. As the buyer, unless you have a 'conditional' clause added to your contract, such as 'subject to finance', if you cannot settle on the date specified – because your loan falls through, or you haven't sold the place that you were planning to use as funding, or any other reason – you will be penalised according to the terms of the contract.

If you can foresee this happening, you can always ask the vendor if they are willing to add time, but they are under no obligation to do so. If finance is looking problematic, this is where bridging loans may assist. Although expensive, they can be cheaper than defaulting.

Phew, we've covered a lot here, I know! But hopefully you've now got a luxe-bag full of hot tips for negotiating the best price you can to secure your property.

It's yours!

By now, I've walked you through all the steps required to purchase a property. With any luck, you're feeling confident now to go out and make it happen, and if you already have – CONGRATS! The next chapter will look at how to keep your investment safe and secure.

● ● ● ● ● ●

GEMMA, 30 – VIC

I bought my first property in 2020, and because it was less than five years old at the time, I was eligible for a first home buyer grant. I received $20,000 in total, which increased the deposit I needed from $72,000 to $92,000. Since the property was $440,000, that meant I didn't have to pay lender's mortgage insurance. Double win!

The day my home reached settlement (September 2020) was the day it was announced that Australia had gone into a recession for the first time in 30 years, which scared me a bit. Today, I'm still living in the property with my partner and, because I bought within my means, I can still afford the interest on the loan. Luckily, I've also had several pay rises at work to match inflation and the value of the property has increased to $650,000.

● ● ● ● ● ●

TAKE NOTE

Sometimes the market can feel so competitive, that finding the right property feels impossible. This is when you should consider less conventional tactics, like buying off market.

....

There are two main ways to purchase a property in Australia: private treaty or auction. Either way, you'll need to sharpen your eyes and negotiation skills to get the outcome you want.

....

When it comes to the contract, read it very carefully, consult your legal adviser and be prepared to negotiate on the contract and the price.

....

Chapter 10

Safeguarding your investment

Congratulations! You are a proud property owner. This is a HUGE achievement and I know just how much effort you have put in to getting here. Big cheers to you!

Now, it would be lovely if we could all kick back in the hammock with our margaritas, but I'm (very sadly) going to drag you screaming back to reality. Dearest property owner, it's not all coasting from here. Unlike other investments, property requires ongoing maintenance and upkeep. And although it's worth it, as there are no other investments you can actually live in (not that my cat wouldn't try taking up residence in my Birkin, if I had one), this is not something you can ignore.

In this chapter, we're going to cover budgeting for property ownership, insurances, maintenance and ongoing fees.

KEY TERMS

council rates: a type of property tax, paid quarterly, that council uses to fund local amenities and services.

defaulting on your loan: when you fail to make a mortgage payment.

hardship variation: when a lender allows you to change the terms of your loan to pause/reduce your repayments due to financial difficulties.

maintenance: the running repairs associated with maintaining a property, to either fix or prevent damages to the building and/or services.

personal insurance: insurance against the risks of death, injury, illness and the expenses and/or loss of income due to these.

Property Emergency Fund: a savings fund dedicated specifically to the running repairs and costs associated with your property.

property insurance: insurance for physical property. This can include home building insurance, contents insurance and landlord insurance.

property manager: an agency or agent who manages an investment property on behalf on the owner.

SOTM-smart property owners budgeting

Luckily, being a SOTM reader, I know that you love budgeting. This is good, as we are about to dial you up to Platinum Queen level. First, let's be clear: this does not mean I'm signing you up for a decade of beans on toast! No, no, no.

That said, in the same way that purchasing a property came with hidden costs, there are some things that just might bust into your world unbidden and unleash a torrent of scope creep, no matter how hard we've tried to forecast. One of those nasties, of course, is interest rates.

Now, I know you will have been smart enough to factor in your repayment ability based on a more conservative interest rate than the mega-low options we were gifted in recent years. We know that the historic long-term average rate has been 7 per cent, and the way things are looking at the time of writing, we might get there very soon, perhaps even surpass it for a while.

This will hurt, especially with inflation thrown in. I don't need to tell you how much the cost of living pinches. Even still, you will have factored in these rises in expenses and have a little wiggle room. If you're a SOTM OG, you'll even have an Emergency Fund to cover the unforeseen – enough to cover at least three months' living expenses should something prevent you from working.

Still, you might be newish to the SOTM lifestyle, or have accidentally used your Emergency Fund to cover the extra costs of settling your property purchase and moving in. If so, there may come a moment when you have no choice but to consider missing a mortgage payment.

Stop. Before you do this, *really* think about it.

'Help, Victoria! I might have to default.'

Missing a mortgage repayment, what's called defaulting on your loan, is a very serious issue. If you find yourself unable to pay your mortgage, the best thing you can do, according to Moneysmart, is talk to your lender or seek free legal advice.

You may qualify for a hardship variation, which means that your lender may allow you to change the terms of your loan to pause/reduce your repayments. Your lender will have a hardship officer with whom you can discuss your situation, and you may be able to request a consideration, which should be reviewed within 21 days.

From there, you should take a hard look at your budget and see if there is any wiggle room to get back on track as soon as possible. The National Debt Helpline is a great resource in Australia for free advice.

If that's all said and done and things are still feeling difficult long term, you may have to look at more serious options. Could you get another tenant? Lease out the whole place to cover your mortgage and live somewhere else for a bit cheaper?

If things seem impossible, you may need to consider selling your property. It can be very tough to get to this point, but realising and resolving this early can save you a lot of legal costs down the line. And let's face it, by this point, extra costs are the very last thing you need.

Property Emergency Fund

'Any ideas, Victoria, on how to avoid this situation and stay on track, even if the worst happens?'

Next to insurance, an Emergency Fund is the best way of protecting your body and mind. There is nothing more comforting than going to bed at night knowing that if, for some reason, when you woke up in the morning you couldn't work for three months, you have an emergency savings stash to fund your living expenses. If you'd like more info on this and other budgeting tricks, I've laid them all out in my first book, *She's on the Money*.

And yes, even if you're 'just a landlord', this includes you, too. When you become a property owner, you not only want to keep your Emergency Fund healthy, but you may also want to consider doubling it. Not only do you still have to back yourself for the unexpected, but your property also becomes a whole other creature to take care of. The sad-but-true fact is that things go on the fritz, break down and go bust all the time in buildings. (Poor buildings, I totally feel you.)

Buildings require ongoing care and maintenance. As a tenant, it was your landlord's responsibility to pay for this. Now, it's yours.

Hot tip: As a property owner, review your Emergency Fund to reflect what three months of living expenses looks like now that you own property, i.e. if your mortgage repayment and other house costs are different from what you were previously paying on rent.

• •

YOUR PROPERTY EMERGENCY FUND

As with your regular Emergency Fund, your Property Emergency Fund should hold enough to cover your living and maintenance costs for a minimum of 3 months. Ideally, you might add more to this as an additional buffer to insure against any emergency arising that needs immediate attention, such as a water pipe bursting. While I know you will (of course you will!) have an insurance policy (up next) to cover this eventuality, in the immediate aftermath you'll need ready access to funds to fix the issue until your insurance compensation arrives. Write out a list of possible emergencies and their cost that your Property Emergency Fund should be able to cover.

....

....

....

....

....

• •

Insurance

Although insurance may seem like an additional cost you can't afford, it can be extremely helpful in funding that maintenance we were just talking about. In Chapters 6 and 7, I covered its importance pretty deeply, so I won't go over all that again, but remember that the best insurance cover is one you never have to use, since that means you'll have avoided the trauma that making a claim would mean. Stress-free lives are the aim here, so let's see how insurance might help.

Personal

Once you take on large debt and/or dependants, looking at personal insurance is pretty much a no-brainer. People rarely think twice about insuring their car, but often forget to cover themselves. If you are already living on a tight budget to service your mortgage and have used all your savings as the deposit for your property, what would happen if you couldn't go to work? Income insurance, TPD, trauma and life insurances each cover you in different ways, as described in Chapter 7. They can make the world of difference, so please look into them. An insurance broker can be quite helpful here.

Property

Property insurance is something you never have to worry about until you're a property owner, so this will all be new – building insurance and damage cover, that is. Unlike personal insurances, they are reasonably straightforward, so unless you feel more comfortable using a broker, you should be able to research online to find an option that suits you.

However, it's not something you can avoid. Your lender will insist on the property being insured, and this is where things can get complicated. Sadly, in today's Australia, insurance has become a very serious topic. The changing climate and increasing impact of natural disasters has seen some properties become classified as 'high risk', with many set to follow, including in suburbs of Brisbane, Melbourne and the Gold Coast. Even if you *can* get insurance, factoring in the cost of rising premiums is a real issue.

What kind of insurance should I get?

If you've become the owner of a freestanding building, you are responsible for it and the land it stands on. As an owner in a strata-scheme (flat/apartment), your strata levies should include the cost of the building and shared facilities, but as a landlord, you might want to insure against accidental or wilful tenant damage. If you're living there, you may want contents insurance to protect your personal belongings and soft furnishings.

Contents insurance. This is one you're probably familiar with as you may already have it in place to cover the loss or damage of your important personal items such as clothes, jewellery, furniture, white goods, kitchenware, artwork, computers, plus other fittings and furnishings. Contents insurance can be bundled with your building insurance premium as a 'home and contents' policy, using an agreed type and level of cover.

Home building insurance. Home building insurance is cover for your home but not its contents – permanent fixtures like walls, roof, driveways, sheds, garages, in-ground pools and fencing. Home building or property insurance may help to cover costs in case of a natural disaster such as fires, floods or storms, as well as theft or other damage to your home. Generally, lenders require you to have a current home building insurance in place before they can settle your loan, as your home acts as a security for your mortgage.

Landlord insurance. Landlord insurance protects investment property owners, to minimise the financial risks associated with renting out their property. This type of insurance can provide cover for damage caused by tenants and their guests, for costs associated with loss of rental income, or legal fees in some scenarios, and protect against a tenant who does not pay rent or any loss of rent due to a tenant breaking a lease. It may also cover legal costs associated with having to remove a tenant for any number of reasons.

Ongoing costs

Owning a property comes with ongoing running and holding costs. Let's go through a few and make sure you've factored them into your budget. I'll also include some ways you can get SOTM-savvy on savings.

Home loan repayments. You should be all over these by now. Don't forget, especially if you're on a fixed rate, that this will expire after three to five years. Shop around and see if refinancing can save you some extra money.

Council rates. Your local council looks after your local roads, rubbish, parks, social support, recreation and community centres. As a property owner, your rates help contribute to their upkeep. For that, you pay rates quarterly, whether you own a freestanding home or lot in a strata scheme.

Strata levies. If you're an apartment or shared-community owner, you will have to pay central fees, by way of strata levies/ body corporate fees, to cover the insurance, maintenance and management of the building and shared facilities. There may also be special levies for additional major building or rectification works, which can be expensive. As an owner you may have some say over these, but if they are necessary for safety reasons, your influence will be limited.

Water rates. This utility is 'always on' so remains in the name of the owner, regardless of whether you're an owner-occupier or landlord. You may pass on water charges to your tenant if usage is separately metered and the property is 'water-efficient'. Improving your water efficiency with slow-flow shower heads and regularly checking for leaks, as well as replacing thirsty gardens with dry tolerant plants, can help reduce water usage bills.

Electricity and gas. The landlord must pay for the installation costs and charges for the initial connection so that electricity or gas can be supplied to the property. Tenants will pay for electricity and non-bottled gas usage if the property is separately metered. If not, the landlord must pay for these charges. If you're paying for power, look into ways to improve the efficiency of your heating and cooling, consider going off-peak and research whether the initial costs of installing alternative power (solar, battery) might pay off in the longer-term.

Maintenance. Sometimes called 'running repairs', these are ad hoc costs needed to either fix or prevent damages to both the building and services. Some can be planned ahead and budgeted for, like a five-year repaint; others may be emergencies, like an overflowing toilet. As a landlord, legally you must fix these emergencies straightaway, so it pays to have an Emergency Fund at the ready. If you have insurance, you may be able to claim some of this back later.

Budgeting for ongoing costs

On average, home maintenance costs between 1 and 4 per cent of your property's value per year. Its age, size, condition and location will affect this and could make it higher or lower.

The most common way to manage this is the '1 per cent rule' which assumes that annually your property will incur 1 per cent of its cost in maintenance. If you own a $500,000 property, this means maintenance is estimated to cost $5,000 per year.

However, there are some things to be aware of when using this guide. Firstly, the 1 per cent rule was originally intended for owner-occupiers, not investors. Some experts argue that renters are less careful than owner-occupiers and therefore more maintenance is required on rental properties.

It's always better to be safe than sorry, so I recommend that you calculate everything as fully as possible and have a healthy Property Emergency Fund, just in case. I'd much prefer you to have it, and not use it, than the alternative. Also – check if it's working hard for you! Is that money sitting in an offset account, bringing down the interest you pay? Money win.

I'm a landlord – do I need a property manager?

There is no law that says that landlords must use a property manager. That said, they can often be angels in disguise. Because managing properties is their bread and butter, property managers have policies, procedures, well-trained staff and regular services and trades in place, upon which they rely on a daily basis, to deliver a cost-effective and efficient service.

If you don't use a property manager, all this will fall to you. Although you'll save the fees, you have to balance that against the time it will take, which is often a lot more than you might have bargained for. There are regular outgoing bills to pay, rents to collect, insurance to manage, maintenance to take care of, inspections to run and vacant properties to fill. While some tenants can be a dream, others can be a nightmare (and no-one wants their beauty sleep interrupted).

Having an agent acting on your behalf is often worth the small percentage they charge and could save you money with their access to trade discounts and tradespeople. As an investor, their fees count towards your running costs, so may be tax deductible. If you can afford it, this is something to look into.

Help, we've separated – who pays the mortgage?

Sometimes, the plans we make go south. If this happens in living situations, it usually involves one or more people moving out. But if you co-own the joint and share a mortgage, this makes things a little more complicated.

'Victoria, who is responsible for paying the home loan?'

Whether you've gone joint tenancy or tenants in common (see Chapter 6), anyone who's a registered owner of the property is likely to be a joint account holder of the home loan.

When mortgaging a property, the lender typically has all owners and borrowers sign the documents. In other words, you must all take out the loan together. That way, the lender can take over the entire property in case of default. If a lender made the loan to only one party, only one person's portion of ownership would act as security for the loan, meaning the lender would only have access to their share of the property and it would all get very messy, very quickly.

Under these set-ups, every owner is both jointly and individually responsible for the full amount of the loan. Regardless of your personal situation, the bank expects the home loan to be paid, whether by both or either of you. If the loan is not paid, the bank may take possession and sell the home.

It is the responsibility of all parties to make sure the home loan does not go into default, so whichever way you agree to make that happen, this should be your priority. Whatever your woes, a bad credit score will only make them worse.

As these situations can get messy, it's best to cancel any mortgage redraw facility – which, remember, allows you to access any extra money you have paid towards the mortgage – as soon as possible. It will be hard enough to pay for your existing loan, let alone one that your ex has increased without your knowledge, and you certainly don't want the bank to make you responsible for their decision to make use of those funds for a spontaneous trip to Bali.

Your lender will have a hardship officer, so if living separately is making it impossible to keep meeting your mortgage repayments, it's worth discussing your options with them. If a prompt resolution is on the horizon – e.g. the house is on the market – you may be able to arrange a pause or reduction in repayments, say, switching to interest only, for a short while.

In terms of resolving your situation legally, that's where a good lawyer comes in. Everything will be taken into account, so it's important to keep good records. Any contributions you make during the period in which you separated will be considered when reaching a final agreement about property division. When dividing assets, it helps to show you've tried to be reasonable and cooperative in the process.

If you wish to keep the home, then you may have to refinance all or some of the initial home loan, but until that happens, generally you'll need to keep repaying the loan on its original terms, pending the transfer of the home – and home loan – to you. You will be reassessed for your home loan at that point, so proving your history of loan repayments will help.

How do I get out of this?

If you find yourself in joint tenancy and mortgage obligations that are untenable, there are options.

When one or more joint tenants (but not all of the joint tenants) transfers all of their interest in the property, the joint tenancy is severed. The shares of a registered joint tenant which are not part of this transfer are unaffected. By law, in the following circumstances, the joint tenancy will end:

- when the property is transferred to a third party;
- when joint tenant A transfers their interest to joint tenant B (making joint tenant B the sole owner of the property); or
- when one of the joint tenants unilaterally terminates the joint tenancy (this can be done to protect the interest of one of the joint tenants in the case of a relationship breakdown).

This is done by filling out the appropriate form and submitting it to the appropriate government agency. In New South Wales, for example, this form can be found at Land Registry Services. This transfer document, however, will require the signatures of the owners.

Ideally, if you want out, the most straightforward option is to sell your portion of the property to the existing owner(s). It's usually a good idea to look into that option, but it can happen at any time – either before the initiation of court proceedings, after the initiation of court proceedings, or even after the issuance of court orders.

'Victoria, what happens if one owner wants to sell their half of the property, but the other does not?'

In Queensland and New South Wales, you can apply to the Supreme Court to appoint a statutory trustee for the sale or partition of a property. There are costs associated with filing such an application, and these costs are likely to rise if the other owner(s) object.

Once the court issues its decision, ownership of the property instantly vests in the trustee(s) chosen by the court. After the trustee's expenses, real estate agent's fees, auctioneer's fees (if applicable), and legal fees connected to the transfer of the property have been paid, the profits of the sale of the property are distributed between the former owners.

Although there are a lot of fees associated with this, it may be the only route for besieged parties to find a way to move forward and reach settlement. Some people can battle for years, wasting time, energy and legal fees and never reach agreement. Under these circumstances, this option may be the quickest and most cost-effective approach.

● ● ● ● ● ●

KIRSTEN, 31 – WA

At the age of 27, I purchased my first property by myself. It was a 1 bed, 1 bath fixer upper and I purchased it for $135,000 with a $13,500 deposit. I work at a bank and can borrow up to 90 per cent without LMI. I am super grateful to my parents and grandparents who each gave me $10,000. Thankfully, I didn't need to pay stamp duty and I also got $2,000 back from the first home buyers scheme. This is not something that everyone utilises and it should be advertised more!

It took me 12 months to renovate as I was working full-time so could only do it on weekends (with a bit of help from friends and family!). All up it cost around $25,000. Once finished, I rented it for $250/week and got a valuation which came back at $200,000! – an increase of $65,000. Absolutely stoked. I then used the equity in the first place to buy property number two. This was a 2 bed, 1 bath apartment for $305,000, fully furnished. I rented this out for $350/ week. This place is now worth $370,000.

I lived with my parents on and off until I was 29. I'm very grateful to have been able to do this as I wasn't paying rent and so was able to save to complete the renovations on my first place. If I hadn't had this opportunity, I wouldn't be where I am today!

I have had a real estate agent manage my two properties for the duration of their rental life. It has been so easy and they are so great to deal with. I know that this isn't always the experience as I have heard some horror stories, but I love my lady! She actually cleaned one of my places after the tenant moved out once. The fees are absolutely worth it and it makes it simple when it comes to finding good tenants. She also attends the strata meetings for me if required, which is great if I want something changed. For example, I am having an issue with the strata manager at one place, so I have asked her to attend to get rid of them.

My dad has been a huge help throughout my journey. He does kitchen bathroom renovations, so his help has saved me thousands. Regarding the building inspection, there had been a few properties while I was looking that were damaged and if it wasn't for my dad, I wouldn't have known what to look for. There was water damage in one property and structural damage on another. I am a strong believer you need to get the inspection done.

● ● ● ● ● ●

TAKE NOTE

With property being, quite possibly, the biggest investment
you'll ever make, it's important to take steps to safeguard it.

....

Just as you have an Emergency Fund because we can't predict
the future for ourselves, you need a Property Emergency Fund
because you can't predict the future for your property. If a pipe
bursts, or you have to take time off work and can't make your
mortgage repayments, your fund will have you covered.

....

Insurances are well worth considering, both to cover your personal
risks, and risks to your property and its contents. Always remember:
the best kind of insurance is the one you don't have to claim on.

....

Be prepared for other costs. Owning a home means a long
line-up of payments, rates and levies. Budget for the ones
you know are coming, and put money aside for the ones
you can predict (like a five-year painting refresh).

....

Chapter 11

Increasing value and when to sell

As much as you may have bought your dream home – the one you can afford, that's right for you for right now – the long-term goal, even if that's 30 years away, may be to sell it and use the increased value (capital growth) to fund the next stage of your life. So, how can you increase the value of your property and when is the right time to sell? Should you hold and use the equity in your first place to fund your next buy, or sell and use the lot to upgrade? When you sell, how do you go about it?

While we won't go too much into detail on all things renovating or selling – I mean, I could write a whole separate book on that (and perhaps one day I will!), I think it's important to remember that, for many of us, a key objective in property is knowing how to use it to increase our wealth in the long term. Let's look at a few ways this might be possible.

KEY TERMS

capital gains tax: a tax on profit from the sale of property or an investment. The rate of tax will change depending on if your property is your principal place of residence, and how long you have held the property.

capital growth/loss: the increase (or decrease) in value of your property over time.

contingency: money set aside for a future event or circumstance which is possible but cannot be predicted with certainty.

discharging your mortgage: the process of removing the home loan from the title of the property, once the loan is paid in full.

equity: your equity is the difference between the value of your property and the outstanding debt on your home loan. This amount can be used to support loans to fund other things, like renovations to the property or the purchase of another property.

overcapitalising: when the money spent on a property, both on the purchase and on any renovations or improvements, is more than the property's resale value.

overleveraged: when you have taken on too much debt.

Renovating

While buying in the right location is a massive factor to your success, you can also increase your property's value by making strategic improvements. Some of these may simply be to improve the value of your personal life enjoyment, but if you're

SOTM savvy, they should appeal to your target buyer too, which will ultimately increase the value of your home.

The most obvious way to do this is by renovating. This can be as simple as fresh paint and new carpets – you'd be surprised at how much they can lift a sale price – or as serious as totally rearranging the floor plan.

On season two of the *The Property Playbook* podcast, Jess spoke to valuer Belinda Botzolis about the ins and outs of selling your home for the most money possible. When it comes to renovating, Belinda had this to say: 'If you want to enjoy it, get it. But if you're just doing it to add value, you've got to take the emotion out of it and look at the figures and the return on your money.'

This has a lot to do with the target buyer in your property area. While some suburbs may come with an expectation of a pool, others would prefer to avoid the headache and running costs of a giant, aqua sinkhole. It absolutely pays to know your market.

Also keep in mind the relative value of what you're putting in. There's no point (unless you're personally obsessed and plan to live there for 20 years) in putting in the most expensive Carrara marble benchtop when all the neighbouring places have laminate. When it comes time to sell, you won't get your money back. Such blowouts are called overcapitalising, and it happens a lot (especially if you watch property renovation reality TV – pass the popcorn). But not to you; you're smarter than that.

● ●

DECIDING ON YOUR RENOVATIONS

Remember your list of property non-negotiables, dealbreakers and bonuses from when we started this property journey? Dig that out now and review it again. Where have you compromised? Did you trade in two bathrooms for one in a better location? Did you put the want for a study nook on hold so you could have a bigger kitchen? The places where you compromised in your search can be a good place to start your renovation journey.

....

....

....

....

....

● ●

How do I budget and pay for a renovation?

Honestly, as I said, I may well write a whole separate book just on this . . . later. For now, let's cover the basics.

First step is making sure your planned design is on target for the area and prospective buyers. Even if you're not planning to sell anytime soon, it's always worth keeping this in mind and is a good sanity check when you're about to splurge on imported gold-flecked toe warmers from Iran. Do you *really* need them? Will others agree and be willing to pay extra for them?

Second sanity check: as She's on the Money always advises, it comes back down to budget. When building – either from scratch or renovating – we're told time and time again to have a contingency budget.

'Sorry, Victoria, I've never heard you say I need contingency.'

Contingency – meaning 'just in case'. Specifically, money set aside for a future event or circumstance which is possible, but cannot be predicted with certainty. In SOTM terms – an Emergency

Fund specifically allocated to your renovation.

Generally, the advice is that it should be around 15 to 20 per cent of your total estimated costs. That said, having this buffer isn't a licence to print money. Costs will blow out whether you want them to or not, so you want to keep this in reserve for *real* emergencies – the reno-won't-get finished-without-it things, like properly rewiring the electricity – *not* the matching set of Iranian gold-flecked hand warmers.

If you haven't spent the contingency by the end, then I, as your She's on the Money fairy godmother, grant you the wish to use it for a kick-arse housewarming for being so clever. (Or add it to your savings. Your fairy godmother would be so proud!)

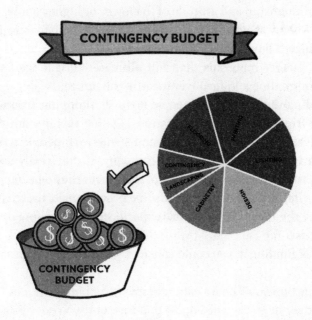

'But Victoria, I've just blown all my dough on buying the place! How on earth am I ever going to fund renovating it?'

There are so many clever-clogs ways to go about renovating so that it's affordable, but they also need to work in with your lifestyle. Some may have handy skills and the time to do bits of the work themselves; for others this would be an unmitigated disaster and best left to professionals. So, as with buying, whatever your strategy, make sure your renovation plan is realistic and it works for you.

This includes finding tradespeople you can trust and that don't try and take the mickey just because you wear skirts. Make sure you get at least three to four quotes. Usually, the ones in the middle will be a fair reflection of the industry standard. If you like the workmanship and attitude of the lower or higher quote, question it – show them your other quotes and ask them to explain the difference. They may well have a very good reason, such as using higher quality materials that will ultimately last longer, saving you money, time and inconvenience in the future.

Finding the right tradespeople involves shopping around and asking friends for recommendations. Online reviews are worth considering, but better still, call and speak with people who are willing to talk to you about the company. If they really are any good, your tradies will have a list of references they'd be happy for you to chat with. You might get some other names, those willing to share their less-than-savoury experience, by following up your online list.

As for funding it, you could consider some of these approaches:

1. By now you'll be an expert in saving for big things. Put this skill to use once again and save until you have your renovation budget (including contingency) before you start.
2. Follow the above strategy, but break down the work into smaller achievable chunks which you can save for and

complete sooner. Naturally, the more serious issues should come first – like waterproofing the bathroom and getting that toilet flushing properly. Expensive curtains can probably wait.

3. Sell some shares. I know we like to save and invest around here at She's on the Money, but it's so you have funds for when you need them. Like now. If you have done your sums and can see that this renovation will increase the value of your property, you are investing your money, not wasting it.

4. Use your existing mortgage's redraw facility or refinance your loan. This is not something to be taken on lightly, but if you spent less than the bank originally agreed to lend you, they may be willing to increase your loan, especially if you've proven your ability to service the one you have. If you're a few years into your mortgage, you should have paid down a portion of the principal and may be able to access funds by redrawing against this. If at the time of purchasing the property, you already plan to renovate, factor these costs into your total mortgage upfront, so you already have access to the funds you need.

5. Personal loan or credit card. If it's not possible to refinance your mortgage and your renovation is small, you may be able to take out a smaller personal loan or use a credit card to cover the costs. Keep in mind that the interest on both these options is considerably higher than a home loan, so unless you know you can pay them off in time, they are not the best option. One small advantage to using a credit card is that it may include insurance or warranty cover, so it may be good to use for buying appliances.

Should I move out while renovating?

Honestly, this is something only you can decide. While some people can happily live cheek-to-jowl with dust and hammers, others with young kids may need to factor in the cost of moving out during the build phase.

If the place is big enough that you will have somewhere clean to sleep and shower and a place to cook meals – perhaps an outside barbecue and a microwave – then you might decide that living with dust, noise, mess and constant early morning intrusions is tolerable. Just. Bear in mind that you will be living adjacent to a worksite, which may present serious hazards. This is probably not an ideal risk to take if you have toddlers on the go.

You can also consider moving out for the messier parts of the renovation, like removing walls or redoing the bathroom, but living through the kitchen transformation to save costs on secondary accommodation.

Ask yourself: if the building works took twice as long as has been quoted, would I still decide to live here? This is a solid test, as this happens a very good portion of the time. As with contingency budgets, projects also need contingency schedules – when unexpected things pop up, they will add both time and money.

● ●

PLANNING A RENOVATION

Brainstorm a list of possible ways you could fund and schedule your renovation in a way that best suits your lifestyle and finances.

....

....

....

....

....

● ●

Where is it best to spend money?

This depends on the property itself and whether you're making the updates primarily for your own lifestyle benefit or to increase the value and interest from buyers.

If it's for you and you plan to live there for a minimum of ten years, you can pretty much decide on what suits you. After a decade, styles will have changed and any decorative decisions you've made will likely need updating again (if buyer appeal becomes your game plan). If you have ten or more years up your sleeve, go ahead and put in that all-black executive chef kitchen with stainless steel benches you've always dreamed of. If your timeline is much less, then you might want to stick to less bold choices that will have a broader appeal.

Kitchens and bathrooms tend to be the rooms that people put most effort into improving, and for good reason – they are used every day and can really change the feel of a place. However, they are probably the most expensive areas to renovate, so consider your style choices carefully.

What about a pool?

Whether it's worth putting in an in-ground pool largely depends on your property's location and how much you think you'll use it. Take a good look around the neighbourhood – what's the norm? If the majority of houses have one, the area comes with this expectation. That doesn't mean you have to have one, but it may help guide your decision.

People in other areas, because of climate and the considerable costs of maintaining pools – constant upkeep, chemicals, running filters and perhaps heating – will run a mile. It's worth you having this conversation with yourself too. Look into the costs of pool maintenance – will you use your pool enough and/or does its design add so much beauty to your outlook, that it's worth paying for?

Other outdoor and garden improvements may be a much better choice, both practically and to add value. Adding a covered alfresco area with built-in barbecue and fan/heater will extend the living area of your house and be usable all year round in most parts of Australia. Spending some time and money to add flower-beds and drought-tolerant sculptural plants will make the place feel more cared for and inviting while reducing maintenance.

Changing the floorplan

This is a bigger and more complex task, especially if you start moving structural walls. Adding a second storey can certainly add value in family-friendly areas, but will hold less appeal for elderly residents. Consider your own needs and the typical layouts of places in your area. It's worth discussing your ideas with a real estate agent and/or valuer to verify if your dreams will suit the market before engaging a planner or architect, as this is a big expense that needs to hold its value in the long-term.

Will a lick of paint do?

If you're just looking to sell the place, perhaps a quick lick of paint and steam-cleaning the carpets will do. A little bit of effort to clean up the outdoor spaces – garden or balcony – can often make the world of difference. You need to decide if the cost of your planned refresh is worth it at all. Sometimes, hiring in a styling expert is the answer.

Styling

A professional stylist is looking to present your property in its best possible light. You can use them to style your home to live in, or when it comes time to sell.

If you're styling to live in, your best bet is to use a professional interior decorator, whose fees vary wildly depending on their experience and the job. They will take your brief and can help you achieve decorative finishes beyond your wildest dreams (depending on how wild your dreams are). By accessing their trade discounts to buy furniture, they often pay for themselves, so if you're wanting help with soft finishes, this could be money well spent.

When using a stylist to sell your home, they are looking to broaden its appeal to the widest market first by removing clutter (your collection of knick-knacks may be precious to you, but buyers probably won't share the love), then by introducing furniture and small flourishes that will appeal to a broad buyer market. The result may be far from what you personally prefer and will almost certainly mean removing most (if not all) of the things that you like to have around for comfort and ease on a daily basis.

This is to be expected. The stylist's job is to make the place look as roomy and inviting as possible. Often they will suggest you remove larger pieces of furniture and clear out cupboards. (Yes, buyers look inside. Remember I said you should do this too?) It might work to rent an offsite storage unit while your place is on the market.

Stylists can cost anywhere from a few hundred to thousands of dollars. It's up to you whether you think it is worth the extra cost.

So, you might be ready to sell?

Sorry, how did we get to selling so fast? You may or may not be considering this, but as I stated upfront, any improvements you make to your home should at least hold that consideration at the back of your mind. In the end, property is an investment. Yes, one that gives you a roof over your heads, but one which should also grow your wealth over the long term.

That said, I'm not necessarily advocating that you sell your property. Ever. You might have plans to upgrade later, but do you have to sell to do so? As always, the answer comes down to your personal values and circumstances. Before you decide, let's look at all your options.

Accessing equity

Equity is the difference between the value of your home and how much you have left to pay on your mortgage. You can use this value to support loans to fund renovations or even acquire new properties.

Depending on your mortgage terms, you could use a redraw facility that will let you have access to a certain amount of cash, or a line of credit loan, where you can take out a limited amount of funds. For a line of credit loan, you only pay interest on the amount of money you take out. If you're looking to add to your property portfolio, you will likely refinance so you can borrow more using the equity you've built up in your first home.

Building equity takes time. It requires both reducing debt and increasing the value of your home – either through market uplift or improvements you have made. Like any debt, there is risk involved, so it's worth considering all your options in detail.

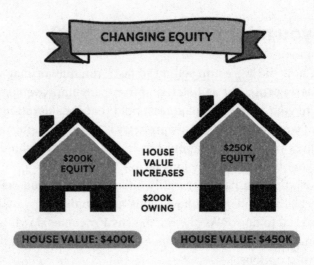

CHANGING EQUITY

$200K EQUITY

HOUSE VALUE INCREASES

$250K EQUITY

$200K OWING

HOUSE VALUE: $400K   HOUSE VALUE: $450K

Make like Monopoly

Over the decade or so since you bought your first home, your income and spending may have changed considerably. You should have made a decent dent in your mortgage, and you may have made improvements to your property, adding value.

Rather than selling, could you lease out your current place to continue paying the mortgage, and use the equity you've built plus additional savings (and perhaps another windfall, or bonus or two) to look at buying a second place?

Now, you don't want to get overleveraged (take on more debt than the value of the investments or that you can comfortably handle), but since, historically, Australian property prices have risen over time and there are costs to selling, if it's possible to keep your original home and step into another while you're still earning a decent salary, this could be a good option to consider.

Costs of selling

When selling property, there are several costs to factor in, including fees from your lender, legal team and the agent selling your home.

Legal fees. As with buying, it's best to engage legal services to prepare your sales contract and process the exchange and settlement.

Agent's fees. The agent's commission for selling the home. The agent's fees can either be a flat fee, a percentage of sale fee, and can include bonuses if it is sold above a certain amount. Costs vary, but commission usually ranges from 1 to 3 per cent of the sale price.

Styling. If you choose to have your house professionally styled, this will cost anywhere from a few hundred to a few thousand dollars per week.

Marketing. Managed through the agent, there will be costs to advertising your home – listing fees, photography, floor planner, copywriting, etc.

Lender's fee. If you're selling before the end date on your mortgage terms, you may be subject to an early-exit fee from the lender. According to Realestate.com.au, this can range from $150 to $1,500, depending on the contract.

Capital gains tax. If the property wasn't your main residence, you'll likely have to pay tax on your profit if you sell the house.

YOUR SELLING BUDGET

Legal fees	
Agent's fees	
Styling	
Marketing	
Lender's fee	
TOTAL COSTS	

The selling process

The process of selling follows a similar route to buying, only now you're on the other side. We've covered much of this in detail earlier in the book, but let's have a quick refresher on the process from a seller's point of view.

1. Prepare your property and research the market

Before you put your property on the market, it's worth dealing with those small issues you've never got around to fixing. Ensuring the property is functioning well and looks good will improve your result. Decluttering, a fresh coat of paint and perhaps a stylist can help. It also pays to familiarise yourself with recent sales in the local area to educate yourself on current pricing.

2. Choose a real estate agent

Ask around – friends and family could have recommendations. Real estate can see turnover in staff, so get reacquainted with your local teams. Attending open homes will allow you to get a feel for the market and to get a first-hand view of an agent's sales techniques, while reviewing the 'Sold' listings online will tell you who's getting the best results in your local area. Make a shortlist then interview several to help you find the best fit, including verifying their credentials and analysing their fees. Don't forget, these are sales experts – don't be afraid to negotiate.

3. Decide your sales method and price guide

Refer back to Chapter 8 for a detailed look at the ways in which you can sell – primarily auction or private treaty. Your real estate agent can offer advice on what has been working best recently. While they will suggest an expected price range, many inflate this to win your business. It's best to do your own independent research and have a realistic figure in mind.

4. Formalise the agency agreement

You'll sign a contract between you and your real estate agent – the agency agreement – which covers whether they have exclusive rights to sell your property and for how long, their fees, and any additional costs such as marketing and administration fees. As with any contract, you can negotiate these terms before signing. Don't be afraid to seek legal advice if you need any terms explained.

5. Prepare your legal documents

Engage a conveyancer or solicitor to prepare your legal documents, typically the sales contract with appropriate addendums. The contract must include the title documents, drainage diagram and a current planning certificate issued by the local council. It should list inclusions and exclusions, the settlement date (or period) and deposit terms.

6. Opens for inspection

Getting ready to list and opens for inspection are a big part of the process. The agent's team will help you prepare your home and campaign with such things as styling, taking photos, writing and posting ads, and holding open homes, which your real estate agent will coordinate. Generally, the campaign period lasts between four and six weeks. Having all your documents and property well prepared before it begins can save you time and headaches.

7. Securing a sale

Private negotiations or auction bids will determine the price and, as with the buying process, the contract may also be negotiated until both you and the buyer reach agreement. As with buying, contracts will be exchanged along with a deposit to make this legally binding.

8. Discharging your mortgage

If you have a mortgage on the property, you'll have to discharge your loan. The process can take several weeks, so it's important to make arrangements with your lender shortly after you've exchanged contracts of sale. There are usually costs involved in discharging a mortgage, so you'll want to contact your lender before you put your property up for sale to get across these.

9. Settlement

Settlement occurs per the contract and is managed by either side's solicitors. This is when you receive the full sale price, minus the amount owing on your home loan (which is paid to your lender), and your legal and real estate agent's fees. Settlement usually occurs with vacant possession, so you will need to ensure you have moved out beforehand.

The time has come

Here we are at the end of our journey. And what a lovely journey it's been.

At the beginning of this book I promised I'd cover all you needed to know about property and help you, as a savvy millennial queen, find ways to afford it ... *if* that was what you decided you wanted. If this is still your dream, you should now have a clear blueprint for mapping out your journey to proud property ownership.

As I always say, it's best to get professionals involved at key steps along the way – Zella Money would love to help, but so long as you choose ANY reputable adviser to help you, I, as your She's on the Money fairy godmother will be happy. I wish you all the luck in finding and securing the property of your SOTM-planned dreams.

● ● ● ● ● ●

JEN, 26 - NSW

My partner and I bought our first home 18 months ago. I would have happily bought a ready-to-move-into home, but it has always been my partner's dream to renovate a house himself. This made me quite nervous as neither of us have any renovation experience, and I didn't want to risk blowing our budget on unexpected expenses. We were able to compromise and come up with a set of rules that suited us both:

- *We would spend between $100,000 and 150,000 less than we had budgeted for a renovated house.*

- *The floorplan had to stay the same (no knocking down walls or adding extensions).*

- *The property could not have any known pest or structural issues.*

- *We wanted a big backyard for our puppy to hang out in while we renovated.*

Over 1.5 years, I'm proud to say, we fully renovated a kitchen, living room and two bedrooms and absolutely loved the process. We did everything ourselves and saved tens of thousands of dollars on labour and also used second-hand materials wherever possible. We have learnt so many new skills and spent quality time together building our dream from the ground up.

I am so glad we were able meet in the middle. This experience has changed our lives and brought us closer together. Not to say there hasn't been a shopping list of challenges along the way, but I wouldn't change it for the world.

● ● ● ● ● ●

So, what's your exit strategy?

There's more to think about than just selling, right? As with any good strategy, the best plan begins with the end in mind, so when, right from Chapter 1, you began laying out your values and writing up your property goals, this final step will ideally have been part of your plan.

Even further into the future, I hope you've considered what might happen to your wealth – house, jewellery, fur babies (oh, and real ones too) – when you're no longer here to enjoy them. And let's hope that's a long, very long, loooong way down the track. If you've set up your structures as discussed in Chapter 7, there's no doubt you will have left things in very fine shape.

I hope this book has given you plenty to think about and lots of helpful tips to help you get a place of your own, if that's what you've decided. If after reading this, the whole idea of property sounds like a complete nightmare, then investing might be a better way for you to grow wealth. If that's the case, then my second book, *Investing with She's on the Money*, is for you.

And if you've been inspired, yet feel this dream is still such a long way off and simply saving and surviving is where you're at, then book one, *She's on the Money*, is the best place to start.

If you're new to the joint, my podcasts *She's on the Money* and *The Property Playbook* release new wisdom regularly. You can follow us on Insta, too, and join our Facebook communities to meet literally thousands of millennials just like you, looking to improve their financial future. I hope to see you there.

Happy house-hunting! Or investing! Or saving! Or, ideally, all three.

With love and moneybags,
Victoria

Appendix

First home buyer state/territory websites

NSW

nsw.gov.au/housing-and-construction/first-home-buyer-grants-and-assistance

ACT

revenue.act.gov.au/home-buyer-assistance/home-buyer-concession-scheme

VIC

sro.vic.gov.au/first-home-owner

SA

revenuesa.sa.gov.au/taxpayer-stories/first-home-buyer

WA

wa.gov.au/organisation/department-of-finance/fhog

NT

nt.gov.au/property/home-owner-assistance/first-home-owners/
first-home-owner-grant

QLD

treasury.qld.gov.au/programs-and-policies/queensland-first-
home-owner-grant/

First home buyer federal support

First Home Guarantee

nhfic.gov.au/support-buy-home/first-home-guarantee

Regional First Home Buyer Guarantee

nhfic.gov.au/support-buy-home/regional-first-home-buyer-
guarantee

Family Home Guarantee

nhfic.gov.au/support-buy-home/family-home-guarantee

First Home Super Saver Scheme

ato.gov.au/individuals/super/withdrawing-and-using-your-
super/first-home-super-saver-scheme/

Non-first home buyer government support

Indigenous Business Australia

iba.gov.au/home-ownership/about-iba-home-loans/

NSW

revenue.nsw.gov.au/grants-schemes

ACT

revenue.act.gov.au/im-buying-a-new-home

VIC

sro.vic.gov.au/homebuyer

SA

homeseeker.sa.gov.au/resources/home-buyer-support

WA

concessions.communities.wa.gov.au/Concessions/Pages/
default.aspx

NT

nt.gov.au/property/home-owner-assistance

QLD

qld.gov.au/housing/buying-owning-home/financial-help-
concessions

Glossary

30-year term: the term of your mortgage (or any contract) is how long it will last. If you exit the term early, there may be penalty fees.

ADI – Authorised Deposit Taking Institution: the industry term for what we call banks and credit unions, regulated by APRA in accordance with the Banking Act.

appraisal: a real estate agent's estimated current market value of your property.

appreciation: an increase in the value of a property over time.

APRA – Australian Prudential Regulation Authority: an independent statutory authority which supervises institutions across banking, insurance and superannuation, and is part of the federal Department of Treasury.

ASIC – Australian Securities and Investments Commission: an independent Australian government commission which acts as the national corporate regulator in areas of financial services and consumer credit.

aspect: a fancy term for the direction a building faces, aspect determines the amount of light and warmth your property receives.

auction: a process of selling property that happens at a set time and place through a public bidding process.

bank valuation: a bank's estimate of the property value and on which they base their loan approval.

bank/lender: though we often think it's a 'bank' that must loan us money to buy property, there are several types of financiers who can assist you with this. We use the term 'lender' to cover them all.

Big Four (the): the four major consumer banks in Australia: ANZ, CBA, NAB and Westpac.

body corporate/owner's corporation: the group of owners who share (and thus, jointly manage and maintain) common property on a piece of land comprising strata or community titles.

borrowing capacity: how much a bank is willing to lend you, based on your income and expenses.

bridging loan: a short-term loan taken out to cover the time between settling on a property purchase and finalising a long-term property loan, typically offered at a higher interest rate.

buyer's agent: professional who finds and negotiates property sales on behalf of the buyer.

buyer's market: market conditions where there is increased supply and lower demand, driving prices down.

buying off market: purchasing a property that has not been publicly listed for sale.

capital gains and capital gains tax (CGT): capital gains are the profits made on the sale of a capital asset, such as a house. The tax you pay on profits from selling such assets are capital gains tax (CGT). The rate of tax will change depending on whether your property is your principal place of residence and how long you have held the property.

capital growth/loss: the increase (or decrease) in value of your property over time.

cash rate: the RBA's centralised control of lending means it sets the base (wholesale) lending rate in Australia, otherwise called the cash rate. When the RBA raises or lowers the cash rate, the consumer banks follow suit.

caveat emptor: means 'buyer beware' in Latin and alerts the buyer that the risk in a property transaction lies with them.

caveat: a legal claim of interest on a property; a notice on title alerting you to the fact that a party other than the owner has interest in the property, e.g. local council may have an easement for a sewage tunnel running through your property.

commission: a fee or payment, usually calculated as a percentage, made to an agent for their services in selling a property, usually collected after a property sells.

community title: similar to strata except that maintenance is typically handled by the property owners and upkeep is managed by a residence committee.

comparisonitis: comparing yourself with others and finding yourself lacking or gloating, neither of which is healthy.

conditional pre-approval: conditional (not guaranteed) approval of the amount a bank/lender is willing to lend you for a home loan, based on their assessment of your income and spending and the type of property you're looking to buy. The exact figure (and unconditional approval) is generally only available once the actual property you're wanting to buy has been bank valued.

contingency: money set aside for a future event or circumstance which is possible, but cannot be predicted with certainty. Basically, an extra Emergency Fund specifically for renovating.

contract of sale: an agreement relating to the sale of property detailing the terms and conditions of sale. (It goes by different names, state by state.)

conveyancer/solicitor: a legal professional trained and qualified to handle the transfer of real estate from one person to another.

cooling-off period: a time period given to a buyer after the exchange of contracts, during which they can consider and potentially withdraw their offer without legal repercussions. The process varies by state, for example, in NSW if a buyer withdraws they will have to pay the vendor 0.25 per cent of the deposit (plus any penalties). Some states/territories do not have a standard cooling-off period.

co-ownership: purchasing a property together with friend/s or family.

council rates: a type of property tax, paid quarterly, that council uses to fund local amenities and services.

counter offer: during price negotiations, this is the 'new' offer you make after your previous offer has been rejected.

default: the technical term for missing a mortgage repayment. Not something you want to do, my friend, as it comes with a bunch of penalties.

deposit: to take out a loan, you'll need to bring some savings to the table. The standard expectation is that you'll bring 20 per cent of the total amount you'd like to borrow.

depreciation: the reduction in value of an asset over time.

DINK: An acronym meaning 'double income, no kids'. These households are generally considered to have more disposable income as they contain two adults earning salaries and no dependants.

discharging your mortgage: the process of removing the home loan from the title of the property once the loan is paid in full.

Emergency Fund: a savings account holding enough money to support you for a minimum of 3 months (housing, food, bills) if, for any reason, you can't work and/or something unexpected pops up.

equity: your equity is the difference between the value of your property and the outstanding debt on your home loan. This amount can be used to support loans to fund other things, like renovations to the property or the purchase of another property.

estate: the legal term for everything you own.

estate planning: a fancy way of describing the ways in which you want your affairs managed and your possessions dispersed after you die.

eviction: the removal of a tenant from a rental property.

exchange: when the vendor accepts the buyer's offer, each signs a contract and exchanges them, which makes them legally binding. At this time, the buyer usually hands over their deposit.

expressions of interest (EOI): when an agent asks buyers to register their interest (make best-price offers) on a home before a certain time.

family: either your best or worst friends on the property-buying journey – all depends!

financial freedom: having enough money to live securely so you can choose how to spend your time.

first home buyer schemes: there are several state-based and federal government assistance schemes to help first home buyers get their first home.

fittings: also known as chattels, these are items in a home that can be removed without damaging the property, such as washing machines and fridges.

fixtures: items usually screwed down or 'fixed' to a property and therefore included in the property sale unless stated otherwise in the contract. They include things like built-in wardrobes, carpets and under-bench dishwashers.

FOMO: fear of missing out.

gazumping: a situation where a vendor and buyer agree on a price, but then the vendor sells to another party at a higher price/ more favourable terms.

gender pay gap (the): the real difference between what men and women are paid – typically women are paid less (for so many reasons there's not enough room to cover it all here).

global financial crisis (GFC): the period of extreme stress in global financial markets and banking systems between mid 2007 and early 2009, initiated by a downturn in the US housing market.

good debt: debt used to help you get ahead in life, so something I consider worth carrying – such as a loan for a home or education.

Great Australian Dream (the): historically, the 'Great Australian Dream' was to own a quarter-acre block of land with a house on it in which to raise 2.4 children. More recently, it's come to mean owning your own home (whatever that looks like).

gross rental yield: a percentage figure calculated by dividing the annual income earned on a property by its sale price or market value.

guarantor: becomes legally responsible for paying back a loan if the borrower cannot.

hardship variation: when a lender allows you to change the terms of your loan to pause/reduce your repayments due to financial difficulties.

HECS/HELP debt: a loan from the Australian government for tertiary education. While interest-free, it is indexed to inflation – meaning that each year, student loans increase by the rate of inflation. At June 2023, this was 7.1 per cent.

home loan (or mortgage): most people can't afford to pay for a house entirely in cash they have stashed away, so they'll take out a loan for it, otherwise known as a mortgage.

inflation: the increase, over time, of the cost of goods and services. If wages don't keep up with price increases, your buying power is reduced.

interest: the amount paid by a borrower to a lender over and above the main amount borrowed (principal). The interest rate can be fixed, variable or a combination of the two. In Australia, the average mortgage interest rate over the last 30 years has been around 7 per cent.

interest-only loan: a loan where you pay only the interest on your loan for a set period of time. When you're paying interest only, you're not paying down any of the principal of your loan.

investor loans: loans for properties that will be rented out. These usually attract a higher interest rate.

investor-owner: someone who owns property that they rent out for income (not to live in themselves).

joint tenants: 50/50 property ownership between owners with right of survivorship.

land title registry: the land registry in each state/territory maintains the register of land titles and manages the transfer of titles under their domain.

lease: a legally binding contract or rental agreement between the lessor (owner) and lessee (renter) where the lessee can occupy the lessor's property for a set time in exchange for payment under certain terms. Also known as a tenancy agreement.

leasehold titles: instead of buying a property outright, you purchase a long-term lease. This commonly applies to government- or church-held properties.

LMI – lender's mortgage insurance: a non-refundable, one-off fee added to your home loan, usually charged when you're wanting to borrow more than 80 per cent of your home's value to protect the lender against high-risk loans. This can be reduced with some first home buyer schemes.

LVR – loan-value ratio: before confirming your loan, your lender will get your property independently valued to assess its worth. This helps determine how much they'll lend you, based on the LVR, i.e. how much you're borrowing against how much the property is worth. Your LVR affects whether your deposit savings are enough to waive LMI.

maintenance: the running repairs associated with maintaining a property, to either fix or prevent damages to the building and/or services.

mortgage: a type of loan where real estate is used as the collateral. It allows the borrower to buy property or land, and is a written and binding contract that provides security to the lender.

mortgage affordability: how much of a person's income is being directed to pay their mortgage – industry guidelines suggest it should be no more than 30 per cent.

mortgage broker: works their relationships with a variety of lenders to get you the best home loan deal.

mortgage protection insurance: insurance paid by the borrower to protect the lender in a situation where they may not be able to meet their repayments.

negative gearing: when your investment property costs you more to run than the income it generates. This loss can be used to offset your taxable income.

non-bank lenders: in addition to ADIs, money-market dealers, finance companies and securitisers are also authorised to loan money.

off-market: property sold without public advertising.

off-the-plan property: a property where the building has not yet been constructed. This could be an apartment or townhouse, or a house and land package.

on the market: a term used during an auction when the vendor's reserve price has been reached and the property is now officially for sale to the highest bidder.

overcapitalising: when the money spent on a property, both on the purchase and on any renovations or improvements, is more than the property's resale value.

overleveraged: when you have taken on too much debt.

owner-occupier: someone who lives in the property they own.

owner-occupier mortgage: a mortgage for a home you will live in, i.e. as an 'owner-occupier'. These are the majority of the mortgages taken out by the SOTM community.

pass in: a term used during an auction to indicate that the vendor's reserve price has not been reached. At this point negotiations may continue privately, with the highest bidder given the first opportunity to negotiate.

passive income stream: money coming in from sources other than your own direct labour. This might include things like dividends, interest, subscriptions, royalties, rent etc.

personal insurance: insurance against the risks of death, injury, illness and the expenses and/or lost income due to these.

pets: always welcome, at least in my house!

pre-approval: also known as conditional approval, this is when a lender has agreed to loan you a particular amount in principle, but nothing has proceeded to final approval. Pre-approval allows you to know how much you have to bid or offer on a home.

principal: this is the loan amount you borrow.

principal and interest: 'principal' is the amount you borrow; 'interest' is the fee you're charged for doing so, usually a percentage of the principal.

private treaty: when a property is offered for sale under no set timeframe, with offers privately negotiated and given a cooling-off period.

Property Emergency Fund: a savings fund dedicated specifically to the running repairs and costs associated with your property.

property insurance: insurance for property. This can include home building insurance, contents insurance and landlord insurance.

property manager: an agency or agent who manages an investment property on behalf of the owner.

rentvesting: purchasing an affordable investment property elsewhere, while continuing to rent in the city to maintain one's current job and lifestyle.

reserve: the minimum price a vendor has agreed to accept during an auction, but this can be tweaked during the auction process.

Reserve Bank of Australia (RBA): Australia's central bank that sets and manages economic health and distributes currency.

self-managed super fund (SMSF): a super fund you manage yourself (with the help of financial professionals, ideally) that requires costly audits and reporting. Not something I suggest for the SOTM community as a general rule.

seller's market: market conditions where there is limited supply and high demand, driving prices up.

selling agent/real estate agent: professional who sells properties on behalf of a seller (vendor).

serviceability: your serviceability or capacity for 'servicing a loan' is a fancy way of looking at whether you can afford your monthly mortgage repayments.

settlement: the date for completion of the contract.

settlement date: the date when the property sale is finalised and the buyer become the official owner of the property.

sole ownership: a property is owned by one person.

SOTM: She's on the Money – my fabulous community of millennials striving to create financial freedom.

stamp duty (or transfer duty): government tax applied to transfers of property and mortgages. Calculated as a percentage of the contract value, stamp duty varies from state to state, and discounts are available for certain parties, including first home buyers.

strata report: a detailed report on the finances, insurance, building defects, planned maintenance, legal matters and meeting notes relating to a building's strata.

strata title: the usual type of title for apartments and flats, as well as many retail shops, offices and most townhouses.

tenants in common: property ownership split according to agreement, with the right to will your portion to your nominated beneficiary.

tiny home: smaller-than-normal dwellings – usually a single room combining living, dining, sleeping, along with a separate bathroom – sometimes mobile.

title: the property title holds a bundle of legal information about a piece of property, including details about the land and who owns it or has a mortgage on it.

Torrens title: freehold title of land which may have a freestanding or semi-detached house on it. It is wholly owned by the property title holder. Named after its inventor, Sir Robert Torrens.

trust account: a separate bank account managed by a real estate agent where funds (such as deposits and rental income) are held on behalf of another party.

unconditional offer: an offer for property not subject to any other conditions (such as building and pest inspections or organising finance). The buyer accepts the property unconditionally. All auction sales are unconditional.

under offer: when the vendor and buyer have agreed on the purchase price and terms and conditions, but the contract hasn't yet been finalised, a property is 'under offer'. Once the conditions have been met, the property is unconditional and then sold. Normally when a property is under offer, no further offers can be made or accepted.

vacancy rates: how many rental properties are vacant in any particular area. Areas with a low vacancy rate are highly regarded by investors.

valuation: a property valuation differs to an appraisal in that it is a legally binding report of a property's market value, undertaken by an accredited valuer. This is usually done in situations where a definitive value is needed, such as family or partnership settlements.

vendor: the owner who's selling their property.

vendor's bid: a bid that is set by the auctioneer on behalf of the vendor during an auction, to establish a fair starting price.

your why: the *real* reason, often subconscious, sitting deep beneath all the obvious, superficial ones, as to why you think and behave the way you do.

Notes

Unless otherwise noted, all web links were verified and accessed June 2023.

1   The Australian Institute of Family Studies research report 'Families
    Then & Now: Housing' shows that the proportion of households who
    owned their residence outright increased from 33 per cent in 1981, to
    41 per cent in 1991, but has declined since 2001, with the proportion being
    31 per cent in 2016. Australian Institute of Family Studies (July 2020),
    https://aifs.gov.au/research/research-reports/families-then-now-
    housing. In addition, the '2021 Housing Census' (ABS, 2021) showed
    an even split, almost 30/30/30 between those who were a) renting,
    b) owned with mortgage, and c) owned outright. Australian Bureau
    of Statistics (June 2021), https://www.abs.gov.au/statistics/people/
    housing/housing-census/2021
2   According to the Reserve Bank of Australia, housing is the most
    important asset owned by the majority of Australian households. It is
    a large component of household wealth and serves a unique, dual role
    as an investment vehicle and a durable good from which consumption
    services are derived. With most mortgages and many small business
    loans secured against residential dwellings in Australia, housing also
    forms an important part of the collateral backing the financial sector's
    balance sheet. Reserve Bank of Australia (September 2015), 'Long-run

Trends in Housing Price Growth', RBA Bulletin, 17 September 2015, https://www.rba.gov.au/publications/bulletin/2015/sep/3.html

3   Based on ABS data, the Workplace Gender Equity Agency (WGEA) announced a series of concerning figures relating to Australia's gender pay gap, per those stated in the text. 'National gender pay gap of 13.3% just a fraction of the real cost on women', WGEA Media Release, 23 February 2023, https://www.wgea.gov.au/newsroom/media-release-national-gender-pay-gap-february-2023

4   CoreLogic's analysis of full-time earnings of males and females suggests it would take men around 8.3 years to save up a 20 per cent deposit for the median value in Australia for men, compared to 9.4 years for women – and that's based on full-time wages. E. Owen (2023), 'CoreLogic Women & Property Report', March 2023, https://www.corelogic.com.au/news-research/news/2023/investments-still-driving-gender-gap-in-home-ownership

5   Workplace Gender Equality Agency (2017), 'Woman's economic security in retirement', WGEA Insight Paper, https://www.wgea.gov.au/sites/default/files/documents/Women%27s%20economic%20security%20in%20retirement.pdf. Human Rights Commission (ND), 'The Gender Gap in Retirement Savings', https://humanrights.gov.au/our-work/gender-gap-retirement-saving

6   *Rich Dad, Poor Dad*, originally self-published by Robert Kiyosaki in 1997, is one of the highest-selling books on personal finance of all time. In it, Kiyosaki suggests that owning your own home is not an asset – since there is no income coming in, only expenses going out, which he quantifies as a liability. However, this viewpoint is challenged by many, especially in regards to Australian property, as outlined by Property Update's Michael Yardney (March 2023), 'Do Robert Kiyosaki's "Rich Dad Poor Dad" lessons still apply? Here's what I learned from my interview with him', Property Update. https://propertyupdate.com.au/do-robert-kiyosakis-rich-dad-poor-dad-lessons-still-apply-heres-what-i-learned-from-my-interview-with-him/

7   *Figure 1: Residential Property Price Indexes, ABS 2021.* Australian Bureau of Statistics (2021), 'Residential Property Price Indexes: Eight

Capital Cities', December 2021, https://www.abs.gov.au/statistics/economy/price-indexes-and-inflation/residential-property-price-indexes-eight-capital-cities/latest-release#media-releases

8   Taken from data provided by the Reserve Bank of Australia, 'Measures of Consumer Price Inflation' as at 28 June 2023, https://www.rba.gov.au/inflation/measures-cpi.html

9   K. Burke (2023), 'The graph that shows why being thrifty is not enough for home buyers', *Sydney Morning Herald*, 2 May 2023, https://www.smh.com.au/property/news/the-graph-that-shows-why-being-thrifty-is-not-enough-for-home-buyers-20230501-p5d4qa.html

10 The REIA Housing Affordability Report is recognised as the authoritative indicator of Australian housing affordability. Details of its March 2023 Report (released June 2023) were widely published: https://www.yourmortgage.com.au/mortgage-news/reia-housing-affordability-report-march-2023. You can also order your own copy of the report from the REIA website: https://reia.com.au/research/reia-data-har/

11 T. Watson (2023), 'How much of your income should you spend on your mortgage?', 17 August 2023, *Money Magazine*, https://www.moneymag.com.au/income-mortgage-repayments-dti#:~:text=The%2030%25%20rule%20and%20mortgage,30%25%20of%20your%20household%20income

12 Reserve Bank of Australia (2021), Media Release, 7 December 2021, https://www.rba.gov.au/media-releases/2021/mr-21-29.html

13 K. Burke (2023), 'The graph that shows why being thrifty is not enough for home buyers', *Sydney Morning Herald*, 2 May 2023, https://www.smh.com.au/property/news/the-graph-that-shows-why-being-thrifty-is-not-enough-for-home-buyers-20230501-p5d4qa.html

14 P. Miron (2022), 'Property, still a safe bet?', AIA, 9 August 2022, https://www.investors.asn.au/magazine/property-investing/

15 K. Jenner & P. Tulip (2020), 'The Apartment Shortage', RBA, April 2020, https://www.rba.gov.au/publications/rdp/2020/pdf/rdp2020-04.pdf

16 C. Francis (2023), 'Major Sydney builder folds owing up to $50 million', AIA, 14 February 2023, https://www.apimagazine.com.au/news/article/major-sydney-builder-folds-owing-up-to-50-million

17 K. Burke (2023),'The graph that shows why being thrifty is not enough for home buyers', *Sydney Morning Herald*, 2 May 2023, https://www.smh.com.au/property/news/the-graph-that-shows-why-being-thrifty-is-not-enough-for-home-buyers-20230501-p5d4qa.html

18 Reserve Bank of Australia (2022), 'How might a global recession affect Australia', RBA Report, September 2022, https://www.rba.gov.au/information/foi/disclosure-log/pdf/222342.pdf

19 M. Kohler and M. van der Merwe (2015), 'Long-run trends in housing price growth', RBA Bulletin, September 2015 https://www.rba.gov.au/publications/bulletin/2015/sep/3.html

20 E.F. Munford & M. Sutton (2020), 'Is owning your home good for your health?' *Economics & Human Biology*, Volume 39, December 2020, https://www.sciencedirect.com/science/article/pii/S1570677X20301738

21 K. Burke (2023),'The graph that shows why being thrifty is not enough for home buyers', *Sydney Morning Herald*, 2 May 2023, https://www.smh.com.au/property/news/the-graph-that-shows-why-being-thrifty-is-not-enough-for-home-buyers-20230501-p5d4qa.html

22 CoreLogic (2023), 'Investments still driving gender gap in home ownership' CoreLogic, 7 March 2023, https://www.corelogic.com.au/news-research/news/2023/investments-still-driving-gender-gap-in-home-ownership

23 The Australia Institute's Centre for Future Work (2023), 'Women Earn $1m less than men & $136,000 less in Super over working life', AICFW Media Release, 8 March 2023, https://futurework.org.au/post/women-earn-1m-less-than-men-136000-less-in-super-over-working-life/

24 H. Parkes-Hupton (2023), 'Inquiry lays bare homelessness crisis facing older women in NSW', ABC News, 26 Feb 2023, https://www.abc.net.au/news/2023-02-26/homelessness-older-women-55-nsw-inquiry/101891388

25 Australian Institute of Health and Welfare (2019), 'Family, domestic and sexual violence in Australia: continuing the national story 2019', AIHW Report, 05 Jun 2019, https://www.aihw.gov.au/reports/domestic-violence/family-domestic-sexual-violence-australia-2019/contents/summary

26 E. Delahunty (2023), 'Upfront and hidden costs of buying a house in 2023', Realestate.com.au, 16 February 2023, https://www.realestate.com.au/advice/hidden-costs-buying-home/

27 The Reserve Bank Board sets the Australian cash rate, which affects other interest rates in the economy, including mortgage interest rates. Australia's historical cash rate: low 0.1, high 17.5; the mortgage rate: low 2.14, high 15.5 per cent, https://tradingeconomics.com/australia/interest-rate, https://tradingeconomics.com/australia/mortgage-rate

28 Reserve Bank of Australia (ND), 'Cash Rate Target', https://www.rba.gov.au/statistics/cash-rate/

29 C. Modderno (2021), 'How to get a loan to finance a granny flat', Mortgage Choice, 20 January 2021, https://www.mortgagechoice.com.au/guides/how-to-get-a-loan-to-finance-a-granny-flat/

30 National Australia Bank research shows that 40 per cent of young Australians are considering buying a property with someone other than a romantic partner. Outside of dropping their price range, buying with another person tops the list of compromises Aussies aged 18 to 29 are prepared to make to get into the market. NAB (2023), 'Young Aussies get on the property ladder "with a little help from their friends"', NAB Report, 27 January 2023, https://news.nab.com.au/news/young-aussies-get-on-the-property-ladder-with-a-little-help-from-their-friends/

31 J. Wise (2023), 'If you don't, who will? 12 million Australians have no estate plans', Finder, 29 November 2022, https://www.finder.com.au/australians-have-no-estate-plans

32 Australian Securities & Investments Commission (ND), 'Qualification, exam and professional development', https://asic.gov.au/for-finance-professionals/afs-licensees/professional-standards-for-financial-advisers/qualification-exam-and-professional-development

33 Australian Taxation Office (ND), 'Study and training loan indexation rates', Study and training loan indexation rates | Australian Taxation Office (ato.gov.au)

34 Reserve Bank of Australia (2021), 'Non-bank lending in Australia and the implications for financial stability', discusses the impact of non-bank lenders in Australia, including a section sub-head, 'Non-bank lending is

riskier than bank lending, on average . . .', RBA Bulletin, 16 March 2023, https://www.rba.gov.au/fin-stability/fin-inst/main-types-of-financial-institutions.html

35 Reserve Bank of Australia (2023), 'Main types of financial institutions in Australia', RBA, December 2021, https://www.rba.gov.au/fin-stability/fin-inst/main-types-of-financial-institutions.html

36 C. Hudson, S. Kurian and M. Lewis (2023), 'Non-bank Lending in Australia and the Implications for Financial Stability', RBA Bulletin, 16 March 2023, https://www.rba.gov.au/publications/bulletin/2023/mar/non-bank-lending-in-australia-and-the-implications-for-financial-stability.html

37 R. Whitten (2023), 'What documents do I need for a home loan?', Finder, 13 January 2023, https://www.finder.com.au/what-documents-are-needed-to-apply-for-a-home-loan

38 Canstar (ND), 'Free credit score check', canstar.com.au/credit-score/ uses Equifax's rating system. Moneysmart.gov.au advises that there are three credit reporting agencies in Australia: Experian, illion and Equifax. 'Credit scores and credit reports' (ND), https://moneysmart.gov.au/managing-debt/credit-scores-and-credit-reports

39 Equifax, 19 May 2022, 'What is a good credit score', https://www.equifax.com.au/personal/what-good-credit-score

40 The Australian government estimates that raising a single child can cost at least $170 a week. That's nearly $160,000 over 18 years and we think it probably costs far more. G. Hunter (2022), 'The cost of raising children in Australia', Finder, 13 October 2022, https://www.finder.com.au/life-insurance-and-the-cost-of-raising-children

41 M. Yardney (2023), 'The latest median property prices in Australia's major cities', Property Update, 1 June 2023, https://propertyupdate.com.au/the-latest-median-property-prices-in-australias-major-cities/

42 Westpac (ND), 'Stamp duty and LMI calculator', https://www.westpac.com.au/personal-banking/home-loans/calculator/stamp-duty-calculator/

43 T. Phelan (2022), 'Costs of buying a house in Australia', Canstar, 26 October 2022, https://www.canstar.com.au/home-loans/cost-of-buying-a-house/

44 ibid

45 J. Mudditt (2023), 'The First Home Guarantee Scheme explained', *Forbes*, 1 May 2023, https://www.forbes.com/advisor/au/property/first-home-guarantee-scheme/

46 N. Field (2023), 'Interest-only vs. principal and interest loans', Canstar, 30 March 2023, https://www.canstar.com.au/home-loans/interest-only-principal-interest/

47 ABS (2021), 'Census All persons QuickStats', abs.gov.au/census/find-census-data/quickstats/2021/SAL80126

48 Legal Consolidated (ND), 'Joint tenancy is old fashioned and dangerous. Is tenants in common better?' https://legalconsolidated.com.au/joint-tenancy-is-old-fashioned/

49 N. May & C. Knaus (2022), 'The Australian suburbs where more than half of properties will be uninsurable by 2030', *The Guardian*, 26 November 2022, https://www.theguardian.com/australia-news/2022/nov/26/australias-unraveling-climate-risk-leaving-more-homes-uninsurable-against-flooding-expert-warns

50 The Australian Bureau of Statistics collects monthly data relating to residential and non-residential building work above certain value limits that have been approved within the reference month and considers this an important leading economic indicator, https://www.abs.gov.au/methodologies/building-approvals-australia-methodology/feb-2022
In addition, the RLB Crane Index is used by industry as a simple indicator of the state of both the construction industry and country's economic health, https://www.rlb.com/oceania/insight/a-record-813-cranes-across-thecountry/

51 L. Spring (2023), 'The offer and acceptance when process when buying a property', Property Update, 26 April 2023, https://propertyupdate.com.au/the-offer-and-acceptance-process-when-buying-a-property/
M. Terrano & S.Megginson (2021), 'What is a cooling off period when buying a house?', Finder, 11 November 2021, https://www.finder.com.au/cooling-off-periods-when-buying-a-house

Acknowledgements

You'd think that the shine of writing book acknowledgements would wear off by the time you're writing one for your third book, but let me tell you, I'm more excited than ever. I think we've finally got the hang of it, guys, this book thing is FUN! I adore that I get to share so much with you and that hopefully, by the time you've reached this section of the book, you're feeling more empowered and ready to tackle the property world head on. There are also a few key people in my life that I need to call out and extend the most heartfelt thank you to, because without them, this book would never have come to fruition.

To my parents, Eric and Judi Devine. Thank you, for everything. Both of you give so much to both Alex and me, and I am eternally grateful that I get to call you my parents. Everyone deserves parents as supportive, kind, loving and stoic as you both.

To Stephen. I can't believe that in my first book, I thanked you for being my partner, my second book, I thanked you for being my fiancé, and now – I get to thank you as my husband. You are the best person I know, and it is an absolute privilege to be married to you. You are generous, and kind, and someone I bring up in every conversation because I don't know how not to. Thank you for always supporting me, no matter how wild my ideas – and being the shoulder I often need to come home to when the days are long.

To Isabelle Yates, my love – we've done it again! You are the best publisher any author could ask for, and there has never been a moment in any of my book journeys with you that I haven't felt an overwhelming sense of support. To the other half of my gorgeous Penguin Random House team, Charle Malycon and Lydia Burgham, you both poured so much love, time, energy and effort into making this book shine, and it is an absolute privilege to work with you. I'm often so overwhelmed at what we've been able to create together, and will create together in the future.

And, as always, to *you*. You my friend are the reason I wrote this book, and I'm so overwhelmingly proud to call you part of my community. Property can be a hard thing to tackle, but I know you're exactly where you're supposed to be, and that the things that are supposed to happen for you will. My last word of advice? Please don't compare your journey to anyone else's. As we've learnt in this book, there are SO many different ways people come to be property owners, our journeys are never linear, and sometimes you don't see what's going on behind closed doors. So, stick some blinkers on my friend and focus on you! Thank you for coming here and letting me be part of your unique journey. As always, I feel so overwhelmingly grateful that She's on the Money has become my life, so thank you for allowing me to do what I love each and every single day.

She's
on the
M●ney

Take charge of your
financial future
Victoria Devine

Creator of Australia's #1 finance podcast

Winner of the ABIA General Non-fiction Book of the Year 2022

Winner of the Best Personal Finance & Investment Book of the Year at the 2021 Business Book Awards

Through her phenomenally popular and award-winning podcast **She's on the Money**, Victoria Devine has built an empowered and supportive community of women finding their way to financial freedom.

Honest, relatable, non-judgemental and motivating, Victoria is a financial adviser who knows what millennial life is really like and where we can get stuck with money stuff. (Did someone say 'Afterpay' . . . ?) So, to help you hit your money goals without skimping on brunch, she's put all her expert advice into this accessible guide that will set you up for a healthy and happy future.

Learn how to be more secure, independent and informed with your money – with clear steps on how to budget, clear debts, build savings, start investing, buy property and much more. And along with all the practical information, Victoria will guide you through the sometimes-tricky psychology surrounding money so you can establish the values, habits and confidence that will help you build your wealth long-term.

Just like the podcast, the book is full of real-life money stories from members of the **She's on the Money** community who candidly share their experiences, wins and lessons learned to inspire others to turn their stories around, too. And with templates and activities throughout, plus a twelve-month plan to get you started, you can immediately put Victoria's recommendations into action in your own life.

You are not alone on your financial journey, and with the money principles in this book you'll go further than you ever thought possible.

Investing with

She's
on the
M⬤ney

Build your future wealth

Victoria Devine

Creator of Australia's #1 finance podcast

Shortlisted for ABIA General Non-fiction Book of the Year 2023

The ultimate millennial investment guide from the award-winning, number one bestselling author of **She's on the Money**.

Through the **She's on the Money** podcast and online community, and her bestselling first book, millennial financial adviser Victoria Devine has helped thousands of Australians take charge of their financial futures.

Investing is a huge part of building wealth, which is why Victoria's second book is all about learning how and why to invest and taking confident action to create an investment portfolio that will set you up for security and prosperity later in life.

Start by understanding your money mindset, risk profile and why you can't afford not to invest – especially if you're a woman (thanks, gender inequality!). Dive deep into the various ways you can invest in the stock market and learn more about property investment. Discover how your superannuation has already made you an investor and get the low-down on ethical investing before creating your own investment strategy that reflects your goals and values.

Covering all this and more, Victoria's straightforward guidance and practical activities in **Investing with She's on the Money** will have you feeling educated, empowered and ready to grow your future wealth in no time. Everyone has different starting points, but it's never too early or too late to begin your investing journey – so let's do this!

She's *on the* Money

budget journal

*Today is the day to change
your financial future*

Victoria Devine

Bestselling author of *She's on the Money*

Take charge of your financial future with this must-have guided journal from Victoria Devine, author of the award-winning bestseller **She's on the Money**.

If you've been inspired by the **She's on the Money** podcast and books to take positive action for your finances, then you're ready to meet your new best friend: **She's on the Money Budget Journal**.

Start at any time in the year and use it to:

- Map out your money with helpful tools and monthly budgets
- Set and stick to short-term and long-term money goals
- Track your daily expenses – as well as money wins and confessions
- Get organised and reduce stress come tax time
- Plan ahead to enjoy celebrations and festive seasons
- Keep all your financial notes, reflections and inspiration in one place
- Complete mini-challenges and supercharge your progress.

Every small step in your financial journey adds up. Using her financial training and experience to empower her clients and community, Victoria has designed this fun and practical guided journal to help you build the money habits that will help you reach your dreams.